DEVIANT BEHAVIOR IN SWEDEN

Other Books by Louis Bultena

MAN IN MODERN SOCIETY, 2 volumes, 1964

SEX AND FAMILY LIFE EDUCATION IN HIGH SCHOOL, 1955

DEVIANT BEHAVIOR IN SWEDEN

LOUIS BULTENA, Ph.D.
University of Northern Iowa

An Exposition-University Book

Exposition Press *New York*

The author is indebted to McGraw-Hill Book
Company for permission to reprint extracts from
Alcoholism in America, by H. M. Trice. Copy-
right © 1967 by H. M. Trice. Used with permis-
sion of McGraw-Hill Book Company. And to
Simon & Schuster, Inc. for permission to reprint
extracts from *The Scandinavians,* by Donald S.
Connery. Copyright © 1966 by Donald S.
Connery. Reprinted by permission of Simon &
Schuster.

EXPOSITION PRESS INC.

50 Jericho Turnpike   Jericho, New York 11753

FIRST EDITION

LIBRARY OF CONGRESS CATALOG CARD NUMBER: 72-164859

0-682-47339-1

To my wife

BEATRICE

*who accompanied me
in my studies and travels in Sweden*

Contents

	List of Figures	8
	List of Tables	9
I.	Introduction	15
II.	Affluence and the Welfare State	25
III.	Crime and Its Correction	40
IV.	Alcoholism	75
V.	Drug Abuse	103
VI.	Suicide	112
VII.	Sexual Norms and Sexual Deviance	136
VIII.	Conclusions	173

LIST OF FIGURES

1 Comparison of Swedish and U.S. suicide rates per 100,000 population   115

2 Comparisons of approval with experience in premarital coitus, Danish, U.S. "Mormon," and U.S. "Midwest" college students   146

3 Illegitimate live births as per cent of total live births in Sweden and U.S.   153

4 Rates of syphilis per 100,000 population, Sweden and U.S., 1920-66   156

5 Comparison of divorce rates (number of divorces per 100 marriages), Sweden and U.S., 1867-1967   162

LIST OF TABLES

1 Certain offenses "known to the police," 1961 and 1967, showing rates per 100,000 population and per cent increases, Sweden and U.S.   46

2 Annual consumption in gallons of pure alcohol per inhabitant 15 years and over, Sweden 1861-1968   79

3 Changes in convictions for drunkenness at various ages, Sweden 1928-65   80

4 Apparent consumption of distilled spirits, wine and beer in certain countries, in liters per capita of the population age 15 years and over (last available year in each country)   82

5 Estimated alcoholism rates for various countries   87

6 Annual consumption in gallons per inhabitant of alcoholic beverages, Sweden   96

7 Death rates for various countries from suicide in 1961-63 (yearly average) for each sex and for both sexes, from 15 years of age, per 100,000 population   112

8 Suicide rates in Sweden, 1900-67, and in U.S., 1900-66, per 100,000 population   113

9 Suicides in Sweden by age and sex, 1956-67   117

10 Suicides in Sweden by sex, marital status and rural-urban status, 1951-63, per 100,000 population   118

11 Suicide rates in U.S. per 100,000 population 15 years and over by marital-status groups, 1964   119

12 Suicides in Sweden per 100,000 persons over 15 years of age, rural and urban, 1925-63   119

13 Suicides in U.S. per 100,000 population for metropolitan counties and non-metropolitan counties, 1964   120

14 Suicides in Sweden by method, 1956-67   120

15 Illegitimate live births as per cent of all live births in Sweden, 1900-67   151

16 Illegitimate live births as per cent of all live births in U.S., 1940-65   152

17 Syphilis rates in Sweden, 1920-66, per 100,000 population   154

18 Syphilis rates in U.S., 1941-67, per 100,000 population   155

19 Number of divorces per 100 marriages, 1867-1967, Sweden and U.S.   161

20 Divorces in Sweden, 1957, 1962, 1967, classified by related factors   164

ACKNOWLEDGEMENTS

Many persons have assisted me in this study, and I regret that I cannot mention them all. They have made the study possible.

I am indebted to the Administration of the University of Northern Iowa for granting me a leave and research funds for the purpose of making the study.

Mrs. June Wagoner typed the manuscript.

Dr. Marshall B. Clinard, professor of sociology, University of Wisconsin, read the manuscript and offered many good suggestions.

Dr. Paul Friday, assistant professor of sociology, Ohio State University, rendered valuable help.

In Sweden I received important assistance from the following persons:

Professor Dr. Birger Lindskog, chairman of the Sociology Institute of the University of Uppsala.

Mr. and Mrs. Folke Bonthron, son Per Magnus, and daughter Eva of Uppsala.

Mr. Torsten Eriksson, General Director of Prisons, and his executive secretary, Clarice Hjelm, Stockholm.

Professor Gunnar Inghe, Medical College of the Karolina Institute, Stockholm.

Mr. Lennart Wilson, governor of the Kumla prison.

Mr. Kurt Tjarnberg, governor of the Asptuna prison.

Mr. Gunnar Marnell, Director of Corrections for Recidivists.

Mr. Vilhelm Karlstrom, governor of the Skenas prison.

Dr. Lennart Klang, psychiatrist at the Roxtuna prison.

Mr. Bengt Gabrielson, governor of the Hall prison.

Mr. Erik Lenhov, governor of the Tillberga prison.

Mrs. Berg von Linde, governor of the Women's prison.

Mr. Voldemars Brivkalns, statistician, National Central Bureau of Statistics, Stockholm.

Miss Maude Helling of the Swedish Committee on International Health Relations, Stockholm.

Dr. Malcolm Tottie, National Board of Health, Stockholm.

Mr. Karl-Inge Elvehedem, chairman of the Uppsala County Temperance Control.

Dr. Bengt Berggren, psychiatrist in charge of the Center for the Treatment of Alcoholics, Uppsala.

Mr. Jorren Erickson, an editor for *Dagens Nyheter,* Stockholm.

Mr. Jan Sundfeldt, reporter and writer for *VI,* Stockholm.

Dr. K. G. Dahlgren, psychiatrist at the Clinic in Malmö.

Mr. Roland Kristiansson, Central Union for Temperance Control, Stockholm.

Mr. Sverker Syren of the Sociology Institute of the University of Uppsala.

Mrs. Gunnel Hasth, Uppsala, guide and interpretation services.

Mr. Henrick Than, graduate student in criminology at the University of Uppsala.

Birgitta Linner, author of *Sex and Society in Sweden.*

Dr. Knut Sveri, professor of criminology, University of Stockholm.

DEVIANT BEHAVIOR IN SWEDEN

I

Introduction

My interest in Sweden began several decades ago. One of the first books stimulating my interest was Marquis Childs' *Sweden, The Middle Way*.[1] Childs described a country which was finding its way through conflicting politico-economic ideologies in a way which avoided the worst evils and excesses of each ideology while accepting the advantages each had to offer. Sweden was melding together private enterprise with democratic socialism and the consumer cooperative movement to create one of the highest standards of living in the world. This was being done in a country handicapped by a harsh climate and inadequate natural resources.

Thus Sweden could be held up as a symbol of hope for those who feared the extremism of a single-minded ideology stretched to fit any and all circumstances. Sweden has basked in praise as the land of the "middle way."

In recent years, however, the image of a prosperous and sensible country has begun to blur. Critics in the United States and some European countries have thrown barbs in Sweden's direction. They allege that there is a rash of deviant and immoral behavior among the Swedes and hint darkly that the welfare state is the basis for the trouble.

The critical barrage began in the 1950's. *Time* proclaimed in 1955 that ". . . sexual moral standards are jolting to the outsider. Statistics show that there are at least 27,000 unmarried mothers. . . . Fully 10 per cent of the babies are illegitimate. One out of every two unmarried women who conceive a child has a legal abortion."[2]

In the same year Dorothy Thompson informed readers of the

Washington (D.C.) *Star* of the "degenerative symptoms" she had detected in Sweden:

> Relations between the sexes are extremely free and . . . there is a remarkable amount of homosexuality . . . they are not at all religious. . . . The divorce rate is very high. . . . There is an indisposition to be burdened with children, or the home is neglected. . . . Except for Denmark the suicide rate is the highest in Scandinavia. . . . Economic stability is not accompanied by psychological and emotional stability. God knows why. Maybe the Swedes are just bored with too much of a good thing. I could not say.[3]

Peter Wyden, in a *Saturday Evening Post* article, declared that "robberies and burglaries doubled in the 1950's and delinquencies under fifteen have more than tripled." He quoted a Swedish psychiatrist who claimed that "many suicides occur over marital and other personal problems because so many people are unaccustomed to personal emergencies in a struggle-free society." Wyden admitted, however, that "crime is still a mild business by bloody American standards."[4]

During the 1960 Republican national convention President Eisenhower referred to an unnamed "fairly friendly country" (Sweden) which follows a "socialist philosophy and whose rate of suicide has gone up almost unbelievably and I think they were almost the lowest nation in the world for that. . . . Drunkenness has gone up. Lack of ambition is discernible on all sides." It was said that Eisenhower had been reading an article in the *Saturday Evening Post*. His remarks caused a furor in Scandinavia, and the President apologized.

A *U.S. News & World Report* article in 1960 carried the headline "When a Country Goes the Limit in Welfare, Here Is What Happens." It then described the storm signals and social malaise in Sweden, where "economic worries are at a minimum."[5]

The theme was repeated in a more recent issue, of 1966, which declared in a headline, "Crime, disease, moral laxity—are all rampant in Sweden, a nation far ahead of the U.S. in providing welfare."[6] It seems to *U.S. News & World Report* that when poverty is abolished so that "struggle is unnecessary and worries are few," there is bound to be a rising wave of delinquency, alcoholism, drug addiction, suicides, and "moral rootlessness among teenagers."

The article claims that crime rates per 100,000 population have increased 97 per cent in 15 years and that auto thefts are eight times what they were in 1950. "The police feel that juvenile delinquency is getting out of hand."

The article goes on to assert that alcoholism is an old problem in Sweden and that it is not diminishing under the welfare state. Drug addiction is said to be increasing, and "physicians say that gonorrhea and syphilis are more widespread in Sweden today than in any other civilized country in the world."

By no means is all the commentary on Sweden negative and critical. There are writers who admire the way of life which the Swedes have created. However, the acrid judgments on Swedish behavior are enough to be noticeable and disturbing. It seems to have been discovered that Sweden is made of sin, sex, socialism, suicide and *smörgåsbord*.

Why do they write it? Jenkins believes that much of the writing is part of the conservative-liberal political debate in several countries in which the conservatives use Sweden as a whipping boy to point up the dangers of socialism.[7] Gunnar Myrdal, Swedish economist and sociologist, believes that American critics are motivated by a desire to discredit Sweden's welfare state and thus to minimize the possibilities of more welfare statism in the United States.[8] He says the critics assume that the welfare state is softening individuals with security so that they cannot cope vigorously with unforeseen crises; sex, alcohol, or suicide becomes the way out. Affluence and welfarism thus produces, according to this theory, a social malaise of idleness and boredom, ruining individual drive and morale.

Whatever their motives, the critics stirred my curiosity. I resolved to find out for myself the nature of Swedish values and ways of life. Accordingly I took a leave of absence from the University of Northern Iowa and spent my time in Sweden interviewing, reading, searching, and listening for some kinds of objective answers concerning the nature and amount of deviant

behavior in Sweden. Wherever possible I looked for the long-
term trends as well as the present situation, and in order to give
the data some perspective, I have compared them with corresponding data in the United States.

A SEARCH FOR ANSWERS

Is deviant behavior so rampant that it threatens the disintegration of society? More specifically, if there is an increase in
deviant behavior, is it caused by the increase in state welfarism?
Many of Sweden's critics have alleged or implied that the answer
is yes to both questions.

Since state welfarism is increasing in Western industrialized
countries, including the United States, some valid answers to
these questions are of fundamental importance.

The theory that a social welfare program somehow produces
an increased amount of deviant behavior is based on the assumption that welfare services, such as pensions and unemployment
insurance, and sickness and health insurance, tend to undermine
the work motivations and general morale of the individual. Living
in a "struggle-free society," the individual becomes soft and
cannot handle his crises when they occur. The theory assumes
that when the individual does not have to face daily work situations, he loses interest in work and lacks the stamina and
initiative to solve his own personal problems; bored and dis-
organized, he is apt to lapse into some kind of deviant behavior.

A theory of the early classical economists was that men will
not work unless they are hungry; whenever their elemental needs
are met, they are likely to value leisure more than an increased
amount of income. It is true that in some underdeveloped countries many workers quit their jobs when they have earned enough
to subsist for a week or two, since in any case it is considered
impossible to accumulate enough savings to afford a significantly
higher standard of living.

In industrially developed countries, on the other hand, many
individuals can get ahead of a subsistence level and achieve a
kind of lifetime economic security. In these countries work gen-

erally acquires a very different meaning: the goal is no longer a mere matter of subsistence but a way of attaining a higher and higher standard of living, so that one keeps working increasingly harder long after subsistence is assured. In such countries it may be that increased welfare income is only a spur to harder work and saving.

THE NATURE OF DEVIANT BEHAVIOR

Deviant behavior is difficult to define, and it is even more difficult to compare the rates and kinds of deviant behavior among societies.

Deviant behavior may be said to involve three aspects: social norms, the violation of norms, and societal reaction by way of stigmatization or punishment.

Social Norms

Every society is characterized by values, that is, belief in the efficacy and importance of certain forms of behavior in the pursuance of social goals. These goals, or values, are of almost infinite variety, depending on the nature of the society and the groups within it. Society as a whole may entertain certain values, such as the importance of education, or of religion, or of success in an occupation. Within the total society there are many groups with differing values, some in direct conflict with those of society as a whole. Thus criminal groups may value certain skills in stealing, the ability to be cool in tight situations, the need to give mutual aid in case of arrest or other crises, and the refusal to inform on fellow members. Certain family groups may place great emphasis on cleanliness, family honor, and self-respect, and on obedience to older members of the group.

If a society or a group is to achieve its values, it must coordinate many activities of individuals and groups. It becomes a necessity, in other words, to establish social control; there must be norms which people are required to learn and observe.

Norms are of many kinds. Some norms are based on practices of folk societies of the dim past. In a rapidly changing society such norms weaken and have less influence than formerly, but they are by no means without effect. Thus it may be incumbent on a person to attend or at least to belong to a church and to help support it. Some ancient norms, such as the taboo against incest and the command against murder, continue to be of great importance in modern society.

In modern society many new norms are produced almost daily to cover exigencies which did not exist before. A new tool or machine is invented whose use involves certain hazards, so that safety rules or laws must be created. New social groups appear with antisocial motives which must be curbed. More children are born outside marriage, so that norms for their care must be established. There may be the development of conflict of a type which has disturbing implications for society, so that things must be done to restrain it. Modern dynamic society is constantly devising new rules to cover new situations and finds it hard to keep pace with the needs.

Many norms are unwritten, indeed scarcely spoken. They may be applied only now and then when an unusually offensive case comes to light. Thus the promiscuous sexual relations of a college coed may be disregarded until she acquires a disease or becomes pregnant.

In many cases it may be assumed that certain behavior which violates the norms is passable unless the individual is caught and found out. Many breaches of such norms can be expected.

There are many norms which are scarcely more than customs regulating interpersonal relations in certain situations. In this category are the vast number of rules of social behavior in polite society called etiquette. Breaking such norms does not send a man to prison, but he may be expected to suffer from embarrassment, and if the behavior persists, he may be excluded from the group.

Some group norms are highly selective in the types of behavior that are covered. For example, groups in the academic field have norms restricted to the limited goal of its membership

—the attainment of academic excellence. They may have little or no concern whatever about individual behavior which has no relevance to this goal. On the other hand, there are groups, such as the family, which have rules relating to nearly everything the individual does, such as manner of speaking, eating, and dressing, and performance in school.

Norms are relative to a given society. Norms of one society can be very different from those of another. Many norms are embedded in social and historical contexts which give them a complexity of meanings which differ from society to society. Theft would seem to be subject to rather clear delineation. Yet subtle differences exist in defining how serious a given act of theft must be before it can be considered inexcusable. The definition of theft can differ with respect to the kinds of mitigating circumstances which are taken into consideration and whether or not rigorous punishment should be applied. Even the definition of suicide differs among societies. Suicide which facilitates the military exploits of one's country can be considered noble, as it was for the Japanese kamikaze pilots of World War II. In another society suicide may be thought entirely rational for an individual who has an incurable and painful disease. In still another society suicide may be defined as against the will of God, a social disgrace, so that the church may refuse funeral rites for the suicide victim.

Many definitions of norms and of deviant behavior may change from time to time; what is considered deviant in one generation may not be so defined in the next. In most American social classes, cigarette smoking by women was once taboo, and violation was defined as deviant behavior, demeaning and stigmatizing. The mores have changed so that in spite of the danger of cancer and general ill health, cigarette smoking by women is now socially approved. Some definitions of deviant behavior, for example personal attack and violent rape, are not so subject to frequent change as are those forms of deviant behavior considered less serious or those more subject to changing fads and styles of life.

Violation of the Norms

Where norms exist, norms will be broken. They are not necessarily broken often; actually many rules are observed most of the time, and the average person perhaps conforms more than he deviates. Even the worst miscreant generally conforms to norms in hundreds and thousands of ways, for example in his manner of eating and of dressing. The individual is processed through a long period of socialization so that in many situations, especially in primary groups, he abides by many rules quite unconsciously.

However, norms are broken in all groups. It is only because "undesirable behavior" exists that norms come into being. Often the infractions are minor, so that the punishment or stigmatization is minor. Many infractions are overlooked as being very insignificant or as ones in which punishment would do more harm than good. Frequently, instead of punishment the individual is simply counseled on the norms he has broken and the hope is expressed that he will learn to do better.

The violation of other norms is considered much more serious, and it may be decided that countenancing such infractions would make the attainment of certain values impossible and perhaps endanger society itself. The individual will be stigmatized for his unseemly or dangerous behavior. Social control, especially in primary groups, may take the form of personal slights and slurs against the offender. He may be mocked and made sport of, and perhaps he will be denied certain social privileges, such as sitting at the common table for eating or riding in the family automobile. In extreme situations he may be processed through the criminal courts and imprisoned, or he may be banned from society altogether.

Societal Reaction: Stigmatization and Punishment

At what point does deviant behavior become so serious that action is called for? At what point does the individual whose deviancy has been overlooked or treated with tolerance become a "true deviant," with action considered necessary? We know that much deviant behavior, such as juvenile delinquency, is overlooked as inconsequential. It may be thought that the behavior is not likely to be repeated or that there should be a certain amount of tolerance for some misbehavior. In the case of adolescent boys, for example, there may be the assumption that boys will be boys and that sooner or later they will grow out of their mischievousness.

When the tolerance limits have been passed, something must be done. However, the tolerance limits generally establish lines between normal and deviant only in a general way. Exact demarcations are exceptional; the lines drawn are generally hazy and subject to change. Whether certain kinds of delinquency, for example, will be considered serious depends very much on which authorities and which police are currently in power and what views they currently entertain concerning the nature and seriousness of delinquency. Sometimes the leaders are pressured by group members to act quickly and with harshness, while at other times such public alarm may not exist, so that the authorities may be quite unconcerned.

By definition behavior is not deviant if it never calls forth negative reactions from society or from within a given group. Deviant behavior is subject to criticism and condemnation in at least certain instances and sometimes is subject to punishment. There is praise and reward, on the other hand, for those who conform to society's expectations. Both punishment for the deviant individual and praise for the individual who seeks goals and values held in esteem by society are designed to correct offenders and to encourage persons to conform to social norms.

As noted before, not all who break the norms are punished. Some offenders are never known or reported. In other cases punishment is meted out only occasionally, perhaps where the offense was grossly public or was performed by someone whose social status is already low. In all norm violations except the most critical offenses, society seems generally to make an example of only a limited number of cases.

NOTES

1. New Haven: Yale Univ. Press, 1936.
2. Joe David Brown, "Sin and Sweden," *Time,* Apr. 25, 1955, p. 29.
3. Quoted in David Jenkins, *Sweden and the Price of Progress* (New York: Coward-McCann, 1968), pp. 12 f.
4. "Sweden: Paradise With Problems," *Saturday Evening Post,* Dec. 19, 1959, pp. 22 f.
5. *U.S. News and World Report,* Mar. 7, 1960, pp. 78 f.
6. "Life in a Great Society—What One Country Finds," *U.S. News & World Report,* Feb. 7, 1966, pp. 58-60.
7. Jenkins, p. 15.
8. "The Swedish Way to Happiness," New York *Times* Magazine, Jan. 1966, pp. 14 f.

II

Affluence and the Welfare State

Sweden has one of the most productive industrial economies in the world. In terms of per capita gross national product, in 1966 Sweden ranked second only to the United States among the nations of the world.[1]

Sweden rates among the highest of the countries of the world in terms of ownership of goods per 1,000 people. The top three automobile-owning nations are the United States (366), Canada (267), and Sweden (204). In number of telephones the top three are the United States (443), Sweden (423), and Canada (340).[2]

As in all countries there is considerable diversity of income among individuals. However, Sweden has eliminated the extremes, so that there are no families living in either superabundance or dire poverty. The distance from the lowest levels to the highest levels of income is far less than in the United States. City slums and luxurious estates do not exist.

The transformation of Sweden from a backward agrarian country to one of industrial affluence has taken place in less than a century, a change which borders on the miraculous in view of Sweden's geographical limitations and its comparative late start with industrialization.

Throughout most of her history Sweden was an impoverished wasteland. She was hampered by a cold climate, with long dark winters, and a general scarcity of natural resources. In the 19th century, when population was growing rapidly, there were recurrent crop failures and frequent hunger crises. Hunger demonstrations and riots were common. The massive exodus to the United States—more than a million between 1860 and 1910— was a dramatic manifestation of the poverty. The class system was rigid, religion was oppressive, and there was little democracy in government. Government was by a parliament which included some representatives of the peasants, but most of the time the grip of the kings and nobility was ironclad. An official investigation into poverty in 1840 chiefly recommended more prisons and a larger police force.

Sweden is a country approximately the size and shape of the state of California—about 1,000 miles long and 100 to 250 miles wide. It is one of the northernmost countries in the world, with Stockholm, situated in the southern part, on the same parallel as Hudson Bay, Canada. Sweden is characterized by long, severe winters with corresponding long nights and by short summers with prolonged daylight. Sweden's climate is made tolerable only by the winds from the Gulf Stream. One seventh of Sweden lies above the Arctic Circle.

Less than 10 per cent of the total area of Sweden is arable. Most of the arable land is located in the south. Large-scale farming is rare: less than 1 per cent of the farms have more than 250 acres, while somewhat over half the farms have less than 25 acres each.[3] Although agriculture is said to account for less than 5 per cent of Sweden's gross national product, and somewhat less than 8 per cent of the population is engaged in farming, still the farmers produce enough to make Sweden self-sufficient in the basic foodstuffs.

SWEDEN'S INDUSTRIAL GROWTH

Rostow thinks England attained "industrial maturity" by about 1850. He defines industrial maturity as "the period when a society has effectively applied the range of the (then) modern technology to the bulk of its resources." According to Rostow, no other country achieved such maturity until 1900, when the United States reached this level. Germany and France did not reach it until 1910, and Sweden did not reach it until 1930.[4]

The proportion of the Swedish population engaged in industrial pursuits was less than 10 per cent between 1750 and 1840. By 1870 the proportion had risen to about 15 per cent, and in 1950 it was 41 per cent. Between 1950 and 1960 the occupational category labeled "agriculture, forestry and fishing" declined 29 per cent, to a total of 14 per cent, while the population involved in "manufacturing, mining, commerce, construction, transport, communication, and services" increased to a total of 86 per cent.[5]

Sweden has a rich supply of iron ore which has become of great importance to its industries and foreign trade. Various small fields through the central provinces were known and exploited as early as the 13th century. In the 18th century Sweden practically dominated the world iron market. The Industrial Revolution in England created a great demand for iron, and as long as iron was still processed with the use of charcoal, Sweden was well able to supply the demands. However, by 1800 English industry had learned to use coal rather than charcoal in the production of iron, and since Sweden had no coal, there came a rapid decline in its iron exports. Eventually coal was imported into Sweden, and by the 1870's the iron resources found new outlets, such as the shipbuilding and engineering industries. With the opening of rich iron mines in the early 20th century in Lapland, Sweden began to export iron ore in large amounts.

The expansion of the timber industry in the middle of the 19th century was more important than the iron industry in the early stages of industrialization in Sweden. Timber covers more than half the total area of Sweden. Several factors accounting for the expansion included the availability of steam-powered saws and the abandonment by England of heavy import duties. Steam-driven saws were built at the mouths of many rivers in the forest areas. Waterways were cleared, and enterprising persons founded companies which bought wooded land from peasant owners. The construction of railroads in the 1850's made it possible to transport lumber products from inland sawmills. The new mills offered the first important work opportunities to impoverished displaced peasants and agricultural laborers.

Although the lumbering industry developed rapidly, it was also subject to violent fluctuations in demand and prices. Many peasants felt they had been deprived of their forest lands at too low a price, and sawmill workers received low pay. In 1879,

7,000 workers walked off their jobs, but the issue was settled by the government with troops. The failure of strikes impressed upon the workers the necessity of organizing into unions.

By the end of the 19th century the primitive forest had been practically exhausted, and the sawn timber export business declined. There developed, however, a large expansion of the pulp industry before World War I, an industry which continues to be important.[6]

In the late 19th and early 20th centuries industrialization was not yet sufficiently advanced to provide adequate work opportunities to the expanding population. This was an important factor in the migration of about one and a quarter million Swedes, equal to about 20 per cent of the population, to the United States in the period between 1868 and 1930. Only Norway and Ireland have lost a greater share of their population through emigration. Most of the Swedish emigration occurred later than emigration from other Northern and Western European countries.

Like industrialization, urbanization was slow to develop in Sweden. In 1850 less than 10 per cent of the population lived in cities. Only from the 1870's on did the urban population grow more rapidly than the rural. However, in 1900 the urban population was still only 22 per cent of the total. More recently the urban growth has accelerated. If "population clusters" of 200 or more are counted, the urban portion was 77 per cent in 1965.[7] "These figures," says historian Sten Carlsson, "reflect the most violent and rapid revolution inflicted on Sweden's pattern of settlement in recorded times."[8]

THE DIMENSIONS OF AFFLUENCE

In recent decades Sweden has made up for slow beginnings and has speedily and methodically built an ultramodern industrial economy. In the thoroughness and speed of the transformation of its economy it is perhaps paralleled only by Japan in modern times. It is necessary to examine a few of the factors involved in the industrial development which gives Sweden its affluence.

Labor-Management Relations

An important factor making for prosperity is the early acceptance of the right of labor to organize and the willingness of both labor and management to bargain collectively and responsibly. As early as 1906, when the Mediation Act was passed, employers were legally bound to recognize the rights of workers to join unions. Among other things it means that Sweden loses fewer working days through labor disputes than most other industrial countries. In 1966 the United States lost 129 working days per 1,000 population to labor disputes; in the same year Sweden lost 45 working days per 1,000 population.

Although Sweden experienced a number of devastating labor-management conflicts in the early decades of industrialism, the last twenty-five years have been almost completely free of such disputes. More than two million of the 2,800,000 wage workers are in the trade-union movement. All except certain salaried workers and civil servants are in the Landsorganizationen (L.O.). Swedish unions operate on the industrial-union principle rather than the craft-union principle. This has avoided a splintering of workers in large plants into many unions operating at cross purposes.

Joining a union is considered the natural thing to do, and whether unions should exist or not, or whether they should have the right to bargain collectively, has long since ceased to be a debatable issue.

The employers are likewise organized, and like the workers, operate as a highly centralized, well-disciplined force. The Swedish Employers' Confederation (S.A.F.) has a membership of more than 24,000 companies employing 1,200,000 workers.

A basic agreement between L.O. and S.A.F. was signed in 1939. It established machinery and procedures for negotiating labor-management disputes. A Labor Market Council was established as a permanent negotiating and arbitrating organization and forum. Since then a number of other agencies have been established to facilitate peaceful agreements between labor and management.

The bargaining procedures are highly centralized. The L.O. and S.A.F. work out general guidelines for preliminary agreement. These guidelines are then used by specific unions and employers in working out their contract agreements within the central framework. The agreements become final only when all organizations are ready to sign.

The workers' and employers' organizations have long since worked out general codes of responsible conduct. They have made it obligatory to negotiate disputes, and strong-arm tactics are outlawed. Contract disputes which cannot be settled by the parties involved are adjudicated by a government Labor Court.

The Social Democrats

This brief analysis of the Swedish economy cannot omit the role which the Social Democratic party has played in the developments of the past thirty-five years. The party, as established in 1889, advocated democratic socialism, universal suffrage, and freedom of speech. It came into power in 1933, and except for one short session, has been in control of the government ever since.

Although the original ideology of the party had been strongly influenced by Karl Marx, and the membership consisted mainly of wage earners, from the beginning of its power the Social Democratic party gave up the idea of nationalization of resources and industries. The expansion of the public sector has been relatively minor since the Social Democrats came to power. The party completed the nationalization of the L.K.A.B. iron mines in Lapland, which produce about 85 per cent of the annual iron-ore output. However, the nationalization of these mines was begun fifty years earlier by a conservative government. The only socialization of an industry which was altogether the product of the Social Democrats was the Norrbottens Steelworks. Such utilities as the railroads and the telephone and the telegraph service have been government-owned since the 19th century. The government owns less than 5 per cent of Swedish industry; private enterprise accounts for somewhat over 90 per cent and the cooperatives for 4 per cent.

Rather than promote a doctrinaire program of nationalization, the Social Democrats are pragmatic-minded about the general welfare. Very early in their regime they came under the influence of John Maynard Keynes and his emphasis on maintaining prosperity and full employment by government management of money, credits, and taxes. The government is committed to maintaining full employment. Whenever private enterprise fails to expand fast enough to maintain full employment, the government must make capital and credit available through loans and deficit spending. Contrariwise, when serious inflation threatens, it must raise taxes, reduce loans and reduce its spending below its income level.

The government considers the creation of the conditions for full employment to be a very important part of its functions. Since the economy is dynamic, with the continual development of new technological processes and new types of consumer products and services, some jobs become outmoded and new jobs appear on the scene. Often it is impossible for individuals to make the shift from an old job with certain skills to a new one requiring quite different skills without some retraining assistance. Sometimes geographical mobility, as well as new skills, is required if workers are to get to new jobs. The government finances retraining programs for such workers and gives grants for such relocations as may be necessary. For example, farmers on marginal lands who want to work in industry or in skilled crafts can get free training plus a relocation grant of between 1,000 and 4,000 dollars. In 1966 nearly 2 per cent of the work force was receiving retraining. Underemployment, represented by working with antiquated technology or working in fields of declining consumer demand, can be almost as serious as unemployment. Both underemployment and unemployment represent losses to society as well as to the persons directly involved, so that government feels that social action is justified.

Industrial firms are encouraged through tax savings to deposit up to 40 per cent of their profits in investment reserve funds in the Bank of Sweden, to be used for economic expansion by the firms when the government sees fit. This is another technique designed to prevent cyclical unemployment.

A high level of industrial achievement is difficult or impossible if government officials are inefficient and corrupt. The Swedish government gives the appearance of being highly disciplined and highly responsive to social needs. It has not been characterized by corruption and pork-barrel politics at either the community or the national level.

Honesty in public office in Sweden is a much stronger tradition than in the United States. Such honesty is facilitated in part by Sweden's having a relatively small and homogeneous population. Moreover, nearly all the activities of government are open to public scrutiny to a degree probably greater than in any other country. All government documents, except such as relate to military security or to the personal interests of individuals with criminal or medical records, are open to the public. Also, there is the tradition of the Ombudsman, dating from 1809, whose agency is a political watchdog scrutinizing the actions of public officials to protect the public from unjust and unlawful acts, and from favoritism or negligence on the part of government officials.

The Capitalists

If the government plays an indispensable role in Swedish prosperity, it must be added that the same is true of Swedish capitalists. Connery has loads of praise for the big businessmen of Sweden. He thinks they are motivated not merely by a desire to accumulate wealth but also, perhaps mainly, by a desire to develop ever new and better methods of production with an increasing array of new consumer products and services. Some capitalists, like the Wallenbergs, have long been famous as financiers, inventors, and industrialists and have power, not simply because of extensive ownership but by reason of their expertise. Many capitalists are cosmopolitan figures who speak several languages and move with agility into foreign trade and the establishment of Swedish companies in other countries.[9]

The Cooperatives

Finally, in this brief analysis of Swedish affluence, we must take a look at the consumer cooperatives. The Swedish cooperatives were first extolled as a very basic part of a middle-way economy between monopoly capitalism and socialism by Childs in his *Sweden, The Middle Way,* written in the middle thirties and revised immediately after World War II.[10] Childs was enthusiastic about the perseverance and intelligence of the leaders of cooperation. Their focus was, first of all, on projects of consumers organizing together to buy food and household items collectively and thereby saving on their purchases. Childs pointed out that the aim of the cooperatives, however, was not only to establish retail stores but also to establish wholesale buying and producing facilities in those phases of the economy where monopoly pricing existed. When consumers united, it meant that they could approach a manufacturing concern with collective bargaining power, specifying the types of goods desired and expecting them at lower prices.

Where the industrial prices for consumer goods seemed out of line, the consumer cooperatives established their own factories for the production of such goods. This happened with respect to electric-light bulbs, margarine, flour, and several other types of goods which the cooperatives felt were monopolistically priced. The establishment of cooperative factories quickly brought down the prices of the large private firms. Thereafter, with the private producers aware that the cooperatives had enough organization and expertise to become competitive if products were priced too high, all that was needed was a threat by the cooperatives to enter production to bring down prices for other consumer goods as well. Today there are *konsums* (co-ops) in every town and in every neighborhood. Large private retail chain stores are also much in evidence. The consumer cooperatives own some large department stores in Stockholm and other cities. It is estimated that consumer cooperatives sell goods to about a third of the nation's households.

National Character

Is there anything unique or different about the "basic personality type" of Swedes? And if so, does this relate in any manner to the affluence which has been achieved? Speculation concerning such matters is extremely precarious; and the conclusions of national-character studies should be accepted only as leads and cannot be regarded as established.

Gösta Carlsson in an article, "Swedish Character in the Twentieth Century," has analyzed several studies, all of them rather impressionistic, in which the "major theme that runs through the descriptions of Swedish character is emotional coldness and distance together with stress on achievement and work rather than the warmth of interpersonal relationships. . . . There is a recurring idea covered by expressions like 'reserve,' 'detachment,' 'psychological distance,' or 'lack of spontaneity.' "[11]

Carlsson quotes some conclusions from a book of the 1940's by Alva and Gunnar Myrdal in which there are some comparisons between Swedish and American societies and in which some references are made to national character. The Myrdals note that it is paradoxical that Swedes, with a reputation for organizational skills, should be found wanting in psychological finesse. According to Carlsson, the Myrdals suggest a solution to this dilemma (assuming the dilemma exists), namely, that

> detachment and lack of deep involvement with others may lead to a kind of indifferent reasonableness in political and social action though it proves insufficient for intimate relationships. The cold fish may be a good organization man but a poor and uncommunicative husband, father, and friend.[12]

Connery writes that among the Scandinavians themselves

> judging by many conversations, it is popularly held that the Danes are fun-loving, easy-going, shallow, shrewd, not altogether sincere and not inclined to too much exertion; the Norwegians are sturdy, brave, but a little too simple and unsophisticated; the Finns are dour, argumentative, courageous, a bit primitive and

apt to be violent after too many drinks; and the Swedes are clever, capable, reliable, but much too formal, success-ridden and neurotic.[13]

In several interviews I raised the question of national character, especially by comparison with the Danes. A psychiatrist, himself quite an extrovert, stated "there is a definite difference between Swedes and Danes. The Danes are happier than we are. The Swedes are too serious and too work-addicted." A housewife who had once lived in Denmark said, "The Danes express their feelings on every occasion, but we Swedes have too many pent-up feelings; we are altogether too concerned about our work." Said a loquacious hotelkeeper, fluent in English and German as well as Swedish, "Swedes are timid, not contrary— just timid."

Connery thinks:

> The Swedes ought to be happy, content, satisfied, delighted with life. Seemingly, they have everything, but it isn't enough. Amid such great material prosperity and the common place tensions of the complex modern life have much to do with the Swedish unease. . . . The Swede is not by nature a jovial, happy-go-lucky character; he never has been and never will be.

It is still a question, however, how many Swedes fit this standardized image. Connery himself says that

> it is unfair to write off a whole people as soul-tortured and claims that most of the Swedes he knows not only . . . lead full and satisfying lives [but also] appear to be happily married and often show a warm sense of humor.[14]

My own experience has been similar; among my Swedish acquaintances relatively few, if any, fit the stereotype.

One thing seems fairly obvious, however, even to the casual observer: most Swedes are hard, methodical workers. One sees businessmen working with their pads and pencils on trains and in railroad stations more or less oblivious of others around them; shopkeepers spend much time washing store windows, scrubbing sidewalks, and arranging their stock; men in shops and factories keep up a steady work pace by the piece-rate system. The Swedes seem possessed by a hard-work ethic.

The work ethic may be partly a result of the Swedes' having come up from relative poverty to a high standard of living in a relatively short time. However, it has also been said that the Swedish national character type antedates the industrial development of affluence and may have been a cause as well as a result of it. According to this theory, the smoothly operating Swedish economy was the result of a rational and unemotional approach typical of Swedes, an approach which avoided the rancorous conflicts that have torn some countries apart.

International Peace

Sweden has been able to avoid involvement in any war since 1815. Although involvement in serious wars does not preclude later development of prosperity, as West Germany has demonstrated, it does frequently pose serious handicaps to its attainment.

Homogeneous Population

Sweden's relatively homogeneous population, both racially and culturally, is another general condition which seems favorable to the development of prosperity. Sweden has no serious internal conflicts resulting in ghettos and underemployment of exploited minorities.

SOCIAL WELFARE SERVICES

In the last fifty years there have been astonishing changes in welfare practices in Sweden. Early in the present century the destitute were sometimes auctioned by the parish to those who could take care of them and use their labors. There was almost no help at all for the insane, the disabled, and the feeble-minded.

Several social reforms relating to such programs as pensions, industrial accidents, and health insurance were introduced in the second decade of the 20th century. The benefits from these early programs were relatively small, but they laid the basis for the vast expansion of the welfare program that has continued to the present. From the beginning the principle was established that welfare is to be considered not as special gifts to the needy but as benefits to which all citizens are entitled.

The welfare program is elaborate and probably more comprehensive than that of any other country in the world. It developed only with considerable debate and sometimes with serious opposition. However, its framework is now so thoroughly established that if a more conservative political party were to come into power, it probably would make few changes, if any.

Below is a brief cataloguing of the most important welfare measures.

Pensions

The "basic pension" per year in 1968 for a married couple was 5,400 kr. (about $1,080) a year, and 3,600 kr. (about $720) for a single person.

A national Supplementary Pension plan came into force in January, 1963. This is based on receipt of pensionable earnings for a certain number of years and is paid in addition to the basic pension. A retirement pension at age 67 pays 60 per cent of the average pension-carrying income for the best 15 years of earnings.

The purchasing power of pensions is adjusted to the cost of living.

Pension payments are available to widows and children of wage earners and to the disabled as well as to wage earners.

Medical Services

Medical-service benefits include payment of fees for treatment in the public ward of the local hospital; three-fourths of the doctor's fees according to an approved rate; costs of services for industrial injuries; costs of dental service; spectacles; artificial limbs; dental treatment for children 16 years old and under; and treatment care for alcoholics in public and private institutions.

Disablement

Services for disabled persons are extensive, including sickness care, special vocational training, and financial aids to set up a business if disabilities permit; allowance for housing; allowance for artificial limbs and the like, as well as wheelchairs where needed; and early retirement pension.

Loss of the Breadwinner

Pensions are available for widows and for children under 16. Maintenance advances are payable for children of divorced parents and for children born out of wedlock. Death grants are paid in cases of industrial injury.

Unemployment Benefits

Financial payments during unemployment are available for a maximum of 75 days, as well as allowances for retraining in special courses. If the person is re-employed in another area, removal and traveling expenses may be allowed.

Domestic Assistance and Child Care

Social and home help can be had when, owing to illness or childbirth, the housewife is unable to look after the home. Help is given at home for the aged and handicapped with attendants who do daily household chores and look after the personal hygiene of the patients. Good Samaritans and children's nurses do babysitting at home and take care of children in day nurseries. There are a variety of medical services for school-age children, free holiday travel for children 14 and under, and holiday camps for children in low-income families.

Education

Education is free, including meals and books, in compulsory schools, vocational training schools, secondary schools, and county colleges. Financial aids are granted for study at universities, training colleges, nurse-training schools, and other educational establishments, including institutions abroad.

CONCLUSION

This chapter has presented a brief overview of the economic and social welfare programs of modern Sweden. It is in this socio-economic setting that deviant behavior and social control are analyzed in the chapters which follow. Specifically we shall be concerned with the question whether the growth of extensive welfare services is conducive to an increase in deviant behavior.

NOTES

1. Enskilda Bank, *Some Data About Sweden* (Stockholm, 1968), p. 13.
2. Donald Connery, *The Scandinavians* (New York: Simon & Schuster, 1966), p. 293.
3. *Statistical Abstract of Sweden, 1964,* Table 62.
4. Walt Rostow, *The Stages of Economic Growth, A Non-Communist Manifesto* (Cambridge Univ. Press, 1960), p. 59.
5. *Statistical Abstract of Sweden, 1967,* Table 9.
6. The Swedish Institute, *History of Modern Sweden* (Stockholm, 1966), p. 5.
7. Enskilda Bank, p. 95.
8. In Earnst Michanek, *Swedish Government in Action* (Stockholm: Swedish Institute, 1967), p. 10.
9. Connery, pp. 352 ff.
10. Marquis Childs, *Sweden, The Middle Way* (Yale University Press, 1947).
11. American Academy of Political and Social Science, *Annals,* 370: 93-98 (Mar., 1967).
12. Alva & Gunnar Myrdal, *Kontakt med Amerika* (Bonnier, 1941).
13. Connery, p. 18.
14. *Ibid.,* pp. 284, 290 f.

III

Crime and Its Correction

Does state welfarism result in an increase in crime? This chapter explores some answers to this question. Critics of welfarism frequently claim that welfare recipients lose the incentive to work and take to thieving; demoralized because there is no need to work and save, they may take to drugs and alcohol for thrills and psychological escape.

THE PENAL CODE OF SWEDEN

A penal code defines the types of behavior which are considered criminal, together with appropriate punishment or treatment. An analysis of the Swedish criminal code should precede a discussion of crime in Sweden.

The Swedish penal code is comparatively clear, simple, and concise. The most important laws are codified in a single volume available to the general public as well as to jurists. Penalties, with minimum and maximum limits, are indicated. This volume, *Sveriges Rikes Lag,* is to be found in many Swedish homes. A citizen can readily turn to the page and subject and read the law for himself.

By contrast, in the United States, each of the fifty states and the federal government has a separate penal code. There is great diversity among these codes in what is defined as criminal and the nature of the sanctions imposed for the specified crimes. What is defined as a serious felony in one state is often considered to be a misdemeanor in another. What is defined as a crime in one state is often not defined as a crime in other states.

The present penal code of Sweden went into effect in 1965.[1] It replaced a code which had been in force for a century. However, the new code was anticipated by a number of earlier reforms. Conditional sentences and parole were introduced in 1906. Capital punishment was abolished in 1921 after a long period during which no offenders had been executed. In 1935 a form of imprisonment in "open institutions" with minimum security was adopted for youths between 18 and 21 years of age, with the length of the term decided during the process of treatment.

The new code is based on the philosophy of prevention and rehabilitation rather than retaliation. It is an important expression of the philosophy of the welfare state. Most long prison terms have been eliminated. Life imprisonment is provided for the most serious crimes, but it is customary to parole a prisoner under life sentence with a pardon when he has served 7 to 12 years.

A few examples of sanctions imposed by the code will illustrate that the Swedish code is lenient in contrast to many long-term sentences permitted or mandatory in criminal codes in the United States. Violent rape carries a penalty of "at least two years and at most ten. . . . If for some reason the crime is considered less grave, a sentence . . . for at most four years shall be imposed." For incest, that is, "sexual relations by a person with his own child or its offspring," the prison sentence is "at most two years." Bigamy warrants a fine or a sentence "for at most two years." Laws regarding various other forms of sex behavior are quite abundant in the United States but almost negligible in Sweden.

Petty theft warrants a fine or imprisonment "for at most six months." If the theft is regarded as grave, "imprisonment for at least six months and at most six years" is to be imposed. If stealing involves violence which endangers other persons or actually inflicts physical injury, imprisonment shall be "for at least four and at most ten years. . . ." Serious fraud, involving a "substantial amount" of money or property, warrants "imprisonment for at least six months and at most six years."

The code permits a considerable amount of individualization in the treatment of convicted offenders. A unique aspect is the system of day-fines which may be imposed in certain cases if the court believes it will be more effective than institutional treatment.

The total fine is arrived at "by multiplying the number of day-fines by the amount of each day-fine." The number of day-fines imposed relates to the gravity of the crime, while the size of the day-fine is adjusted to the offender's capacity to pay. The day-fine system is an example of Swedish democracy in operation. If a simple assault is assessed 10 day-fines, then for a wealthy person who earns 300 crowns a day the fine would be 10 times 300, or 3,000, crowns; for a poor man earning 20 crowns a day it would be 10 times 20, or 200, crowns for the same offense.

The Code specifies a wide range of possible lengths of sentences. The court has to judge the relative seriousness of a given crime—whether it has violent overtones, whether anyone was actually injured, the nature of the offender's record—and pronounce sentence accordingly. The actual treatment is determined altogether by correctional authorities, who decide, for example, whether the offender should be placed in an "open" or a "closed" institution and what kind of training he should receive. Every institution has a Supervision Board presided over by a judge. This Board has full authority to grant conditional liberation or early release.

If a person is guilty of several offenses, and if his "mental condition, conduct and other circumstances" warrant it, the court may impose treatment without fixing the duration in advance. Such treatment begins in an institution but may be continued outside institutions. As a rule the court fixes a minimum time of one year and a maximum of twelve years for custodial institutional care for such recidivist cases. The Internment Board has broad powers to release a prisoner after one year or to hold him beyond the maximum if it can convince the court that this is necessary.

The Code does not exempt feeble-minded or mentally ill defendants from all sanctions. There is no statement that such offenders may lack the ability to know whether they have committed a wrong or acted against the law. The Code only limits the sanctions which can be applied. Imprisonment and conditional sentences cannot be used. Most commonly such offenders are committed to a mental hospital or to open psychiatric care. Sometimes probationary care is provided or fines may be levied. The

Swedish Code has abandoned the doctrine that there are two classes of persons, the responsible and the irresponsible, and that the second class must be exempt from justice. Since punishment has been completely eliminated as a motive for the official processing of offenders, the logic of all official sentences is treatment of the individual on the basis of his personal traits, and only secondarily, if at all, on the basis of the particular crime he has committed. The specific crime committed can be relevant only to the degree that it gives a clue to the personality of the offender.

A sentence to a youth prison may be imposed on persons between the ages of 18 and 23. Some of the youth institutions are closed, others are open, while still others have both open and closed sections. The Code prescribes that youth prisons must place special emphasis on education and vocational training.

Although there are some serious offenses, such as drunken driving, for which a youth under 18 years of age may be imprisoned, more generally persons under 18 are turned over to child welfare agencies.

The Swedish penal code is pragmatic. It has no slavish adherence to some philosophical theory of human nature and motivations; it seeks practical ways for the rehabilitation of offenders. There is no emphasis on laws against individual behavior of a kind that has little or no relevance to the welfare of others. Its sanctions are relatively mild and in most cases non-institutional.

THE AMOUNT OF CRIME

The Statistical Record

It is impossible to know with any exactness how much crime exists within a given society at a given time. To begin with, there are crimes which are not known or discovered by the police and the courts.

However, "crimes known to the police" is generally regarded as the best available index of crime. Many offenders are never discovered or arrested, although police may know of their crimes through complaints by victims and witnesses or through the process of their own operations. Not all crimes are discovered or reported. There are witnesses who want to "stay out of trouble," and there are victims who are intimidated or who receive private recompense from the offenders. Moreover, it makes a difference how thoroughly the police keep their records. Some complaints may not seem worth recording by some police but may all go into the records of other police. Another variable is the relative vigilance of the police in their patrols and search for criminal offenses. Obviously relevant here is the size of the police force in relation to the population and the quality of its training and experience. Sometimes a change in police administration in a given city or country may produce an apparent rise or fall in the crime rates because of the differences in conscientiousness of the recording of complaints and in the interpretations of borderline cases regarding whether they constitute criminal or non-criminal behavior.

To compare the amount of crime among jurisdictions is complicated by the differences in the way crimes are defined. This is especially so when comparisons are made between two countries with many differences in values and ways of life. In addition, many acts which are labeled as criminal behavior in one society may not be so defined in another. I have found only a few categories in the United States and Swedish crime statistics which seem fairly similar and comparable. There is the problem of defining exactly what is meant by such terms as "offense against the state," "breach of the peace," "disorderly conduct," and "cruelty to animals." How serious must an "assault upon the person" be to meet the specifications of criminal behavior? These, and many other forms of behavior, are rigidly defined in some societies and loosely in others. The judges of courts applying the same criminal code often make vastly different judgments concerning what behavior is considered criminal and what sanctions should be applied.[2]

A dependable gauge of the amount of crime and of crime trends does not exist. However, "crimes known to the police" is generally considered to be a better index of crime than any other index available.

Every country has crime which is not known to the police or other authorities. There is reason to believe that such unknown crime is at a considerably higher rate in the United States than in Sweden. In the United States the complexity of state and federal laws, the large city ghettos, the fractured police system, the powerful crime syndicates, and the failure of victims to report offenses mean that "crimes known to the police" are only a fraction of the crimes actually committed. On the basis of surveys of unreported crime by the Bureau of Social Science Research of Washington, D.C., the Survey Research Center of the University of Michigan, and the National Opinion Research Center of the University of Chicago, the President's Commission on Law Enforcement and the Administration of Justice concludes that "the actual amount of crime in the United States today is several times that reported in the uniform Crime Reports."[3] There is secret crime in Sweden, too; however, because the country is relatively small, and because the laws and police system are less complicated, and crime syndicates are non-existent, the crime known to the police is probably closer to the real rate than is the case in the United States.

The arrest rate is less accurate as a crime index, since many crimes are known for which no arrests are ever made. Police may be aware that certain break-ins and robberies have taken place but may never have enough evidence or clues to lead to an arrest. In 1967, of 2,192,808 serious crimes known to the police in the United States, only 20 per cent led to arrests. Of those arrested, only 75 per cent were charged and of those charged, only 71 per cent were convicted.[4] From this it is also obvious that the number of persons imprisoned or otherwise punished is even less accurate as an index of crime rates.

The data available reports considerable increases in crime rates in both the United States and Sweden.

Table 1 compares the incidence of certain types of crimes "known to the police" in Sweden and in the United States in 1961 and 1967. In both countries crimes of these types increased, though the rate of increase was considerable higher in the United States than in Sweden. For all categories except auto theft, the incidence rate was considerably higher in 1961 and in 1967 in the United States than in Sweden. For "murder and manslaughter" the rate was three times as high, for rape it was about twice as high, and for robbery 10 times as high. For auto theft the rates for the two countries in 1967 were about the same.

The highest rate of arrest and conviction among all crimes known to the police is generally for murder. There is reason to believe that the murder rate in Sweden is very low. In 1966 the Swedish courts sentenced only five persons for murder, a rate of .06 per 100,000 population. In the United States, 3,617 were convicted of murder in 1967, a rate of 1.8 per 100,000 population, 30 times the Swedish rate.

To compare the rates of the several categories in Table 1, it is necessary to give definitions of the crimes classified as used in

TABLE 1

Certain Offenses "Known to the Police," 1961 & 1967, Showing Rates Per 100,000 Population and Per Cent Increases, Sweden and U.S.

SWEDEN

OFFENSE	1961	RATE	1967	RATE	PER CENT INCREASE
MURDER AND MANSLAUGHTER	127	1.7	172	2.2	29
RAPE	516	6.8	652	8.3	22
ROBBERY	491	6.5	1,034	13.1	102
AUTO THEFT	20,968	278.1	30,198	382.7	38

UNITED STATES

OFFENSE	1961	RATE	1967	RATE	PER CENT INCREASE
MURDER AND MANSLAUGHTER	8,630	4.7	13,648	6.8	45
RAPE	16,890	9.2	31,057	15.5	68
ROBBERY	103,580	56.6	261,728	131.0	131
AUTO THEFT	333,500	182.3	777,755	389.1	113

Sources: Sweden: **Statistical Abstract of Sweden, 1969,** Table 318, "Offenses Known to the Police."
U.S.: FBI **Uniform Crime Reports, 1968,** Tables 1 & 2.

the United States and in Sweden. They are by no means the same. Thus there is an uncertain line between murder and manslaughter, and which particular criminal killing is defined as murder and which as manslaughter depends very much on the penal code and on the interpretation by police and the courts.

*Definitions**

Murder and Manslaughter

Sweden: Murder is "taking the life of another"; when, in the judgment of the court, "the crime is less grave" it is defined as manslaughter.

United States: "Includes all willful killings . . . scored on the basis of police investigation . . . deaths caused by negligence . . . are counted as manslaughter by negligence."

Rape

Sweden: An act in which "a man by violence or threat . . . forces a woman to have sexual intercourse."

United States: ". . . carnal knowledge of a female forcibly and against her will. Assaults to rape are also included; however, statutory rape without force is not counted."

Robbery

Sweden: Stealing "by means of violence . . . or by means of threat implying imminent danger."

United States: ". . . stealing . . . of anything of value from the person by force or threat of force. Assaults to rob and attempts are included."

Auto Theft

Sweden: ". . . unlawfully taking or using a motor vehicle."

United States: ". . . the unlawful stealing or driving away of a motor vehicle, including attempts."

---

*Sources: Sweden: *The Penal Code*.

         United States: FBI *Uniform Crime Reports, 1967*.

Professor Knut Sveri on Organized Crime

In an extensive interview I asked Professor of Criminology Knut Sveri of the University of Stockholm if Sweden had any professional criminals, that is, criminals who were highly skilled and specialized, enjoy high status in the underworld and make their living by crime. He said:

> There are relatively few professional criminals in Sweden. However, there are some thieves who do make a living by thieving and to some degree approximate the professional type. There is little, if any, opportunity for such thieves to be strongly organized and to buy off the police and local officials.
>
> Probably the thieves in Sweden who come closest to the professional type are those who break safes by dynamite or by acetylene torches. There are about 150 cases a year of this kind of stealing in Stockholm. I have made a study of 25 such thieves in our prisons. In order to be included in my sample they had to be over 20 years of age and involved in thieving for at least five years. At least one of the men had purposely learned to use an acetylene torch while in prison, a skill which he later applied to opening safes.
>
> Most of the men in the sample are older than the average prisoner. They are definitely "outsiders"; they are alienated from society and generally from their families and relatives. They score high on intelligence tests. Only two of them are from homes which had not been broken at some time when they were children.
>
> These young men are not as completely professional as the thieves Sutherland[5] writes about. They do not specialize altogether in stealing from safes; they have a tendency to participate in other kinds of stealing as well.
>
> There is no evidence of a Mafia or Cosa Nostra type of crime syndicate in Sweden, an organization which plays such a prominent part in the rackets in the United States. The big crime syndicates in the United States are heavily dependent on political and police protection. I think there are several reasons for the lack of crime organizations in Sweden.
>
> There is more honesty among police and public officials in Sweden than has traditionally been the case in the United States. There are various private-citizen groups, plus the ever-vigilant office of the Ombudsmen, who keep a careful watch over police and political figures to keep them honest. The government of

Sweden is, of course, smaller and less complex than the government of the United States. The conduct of a public official is relatively more open to view, so that it is harder for him to commit offenses against the public trust. Moreover, businessmen are relatively honest. Thus, in the case of advertising, consumer complaints are more likely to lead to corrections under pressures from governmental agencies and from the large consumer organizations themselves than is the case in the United States. There is not the big gap between consumer interests and business interests which exists in some countries.

Moreover, Sweden has an integrated national police force, well trained and with high qualifications, in contrast to the fragmented police systems of the federal government, the states, and the metropolitan regions of the United States. Every Swedish community has a citizens' organization which has the task of keeping itself informed on police problems and functions in its area. It is very difficult, if not impossible, to buy off the police for special protection of racket syndicates, a protection without which such syndicates could not function.

It should be added that the opportunities to engage in illegal gambling and prostitution, two very lucrative rackets in the United States, are non-existent in Sweden. Both gambling and prostitution are legal and regulated. To be a pimp for prostitutes is a criminal matter, as is also the use of force compelling a woman to submit to sexual relations. It is also illegal for a man to take advantage of a girl under 15. Health and welfare authorities may be concerned about the health problems of prostitutes and what commercial sex may do to a woman's morale and status. However, prostitution in itself is not illegal. If a woman agrees to take money or favors for sex, this is her own affair.

Personal Impressions

Some personal impressions concerning crime in Sweden may be in order. I traveled in various areas and cities of Sweden, but most of my time was spent in Uppsala and in the Stockholm region.

At Uppsala University, with 20,000 students, I often noted that students deposited their books and other belongings in open cloakrooms while going to classes or lunch. There seemed to be no fear of theft. Likewise, in the restaurants of Stockholm patrons left garments and packages in public cloakrooms. Sometimes they left purses and handbags on tables or chairs while joining a cafeteria lineup. One Sunday a group of eight or ten "classic automobiles" drove to a rural restaurant. When the occupants went into the restaurant, they left handbags and cameras lying on the seats of the cars, which were open with tops down. This was done in spite of there being forty or fifty curious people crowding around to examine the cars. Numerous incidents similar to these could be recounted. It is hard to avoid the distinct impression that the rate of casual larceny must be considerably lower than in the United States.

Youth Crime

As in many other countries, there has been a serious increase in youth crime in Sweden in the past ten or fifteen years. The most important criminal behavior includes theft, such as petty larceny and car stealing, vandalism, sex offenses, the abuse of drugs and alcohol, truancy, and disciplinary difficulties at school.

Many social changes relate to the increase in delinquency. There has been a rural depopulation that has transformed Sweden into a highly urbanized country in a relatively short time. Home and family life have changed. An increasing proportion of mothers are gainfully employed. Many of the earlier tasks, such as laundering, baking, and preserving food, once performed largely by the family are now performed mostly outside the home. Children have fewer farm and home chores, and they spend longer years in school. There is generally a considerable amount of leisure outside of school hours.

Youth now have more freedom of choice concerning careers, interests, and marriage partners. Doors have been opened to larger opportunities. But these developments have also enhanced the risks. Youths now have more money than ever before; the "hot-rod set" is evident in every town, particularly on week ends. "Differential association" among problem children is now more readily possible than formerly. Delinquent subcultures facilitate delinquency and crime.

In several important respects, however, the situation with respect to youth crime is drastically different from that in the United States. Sweden has a relatively homogeneous population. There have been no successive waves of immigrants into the cities such as occurred in the United States in the last decades of the 19th century and the early decades of the 20th. Waves of immigrants into the United States often led to culture conflicts and a cramming into city slums. As more newcomers came and took the lower rungs of the social ladder, the earlier comers were generally able to move into better parts of the cities or into the suburbs. Many of the most recent migrants to the cities, the Negroes and the Puerto Ricans, are now walled in the ghettos with almost nowhere else to go.

One of the by-products of the successive waves of newcomers, who had previously lived mostly in villages, was family and community breakdown and the development of juvenile gangs. This is documented by numerous studies.[6]

Youth crime in the United States is to a considerable degree a city slum product and a phenomenon of working and unemployed classes.[7] Gangs function as aggressive play groups and give some social security to boys who have little of it at home or at school. The play activity of the gangs now and then spills over into crime, with theft, vandalism, drinking, sex sprees, and gang warfare. The gang warfare is sometimes interethnic and/or interracial.

Sweden has a big advantage in the control of youth crime in that it has no city slums or significant racial or ethnic minority conflicts. There are some semi-Bohemian areas in the large cities, however, where subcultures centering on drug abuse and nonconformity have developed.

Gun Control

Sweden has relatively low rates for crimes of violence. In 1967 robbery, as "known to the police," was at a rate of 13.1 per 100,000 population. In the same year it was 78.3 per 100,000 in the United States. As previously noted, murder rates in Sweden are comparatively very low.

Explanations for these differences are no doubt many and complex. One item of some significance, I believe, is Sweden's tight gun-control law in contrast to the almost complete absence of gun control in the United States.

You cannot obtain a gun in Sweden unless you can demonstrate that you know how to use it and for what purposes it is to be used. If you propose to hunt, you must prove that you own land or have access to land where hunting may take place. In addition, you must give acceptable evidence of being a stable person and a citizen of good repute.

Vilhelm Karlstrom, governor of the Skenas prison, stated:

> . . . military guns are hidden in caches in a great variety of places in Sweden. These are available to local army units in case of invasion. In recent years it has happened several times that young men have broken into some of these caches and stolen the guns. When this has happened, and until the police recaptured the guns, there have occurred more crimes of violence or threats of violence, as in robbery, involving the use of guns. For a few years there appeared the *stelleto* knife, and it was used in a number of crimes. However, the authorities pounced on this weapon very severely, so that the knives are no longer available in Sweden. Robbery is sometimes committed with no weapon but with superior physical force or with the threat of such force. It seems evident that Sweden's strict gun-control law diminishes the opportunity and occurrence of robberies and other crimes involving violence. Bank holdups, for example, are comparatively rare in Sweden. The lack of guns is not the only explanation for this, but it can be stated that guns greatly facilitate bank robberies and that in fact such robberies are almost impossible without guns.

In the United States in 1967 firearms were used to commit 7,600 murders (63% of the total), 52,000 aggravated assaults, and 73,000 robberies.[8] We do not know how many of these crimes of violence would have happened without guns, but a gun is a quick effective weapon and facilitates violence. One may hypothesize that many a murder in a family or neighborhood (most murders in the United States are of relatives, friends, neighbors, and acquaintances) in the midst of an emotional altercation probably would not happen if it were not for a gun being available.

It is impossible to measure the amount of crime in a given country and to compare the rates of crime in several countries with anything approaching statistical precision. However, both statistical data and general impressions support the generalization that the rate of serious crimes in Sweden is probably considerably lower than rates in the United States. Some of the probable reasons for this difference have been mentioned: a more homogeneous population, a unified penal code, a national police force, a long-time tradition of a non-violent approach to life, less internal migration and less immigration from abroad, a long-time tradition of honesty in public office, and a lack of opportunity for the development or organized crime syndicates of the American variety.

Probably Sweden's humane and enlightened correctional system, described below, also relates to a lower rate of crime. In the United States it seems that prisons often are as much a cause of crime as a cure for crime.

THE CORRECTIONAL SYSTEM OF SWEDEN

Size of Prisons

I visited ten prisons with opportunity to see all the facilities and programs and to converse with staff and inmates. Each prison was a different type, and the ten represented a cross section of the 80 prisons of Sweden. At any one time Sweden has about 5,000 persons in prison, including about 500 who are detained pending trial. The figure does not include persons arrested and held in custody by the police, which custody is limited to a maximum of four days.

The average prison is small, with about 60 inmates. Some American prisons hold as many as four or five thousand inmates.

Anyone who has visited American prisons knows how the inmates are almost constantly exposed to a mass environment. Work generally involves situations where large numbers are together. Yard exercises and athletic programs likewise are typically planned for the many rather than for a few in isolated privacy. Eating is in huge dining rooms. The typical American inmate does not even have privacy in his cell. Not only are many prisons crowded with two or even three men per cell, but the cells have bars rather than doors, so that the inmates are exposed to the view of other inmates and of the guards. Even at night when lights are turned off there can be little sense of privacy. There are noises of men talking, arguing, snoring and coughing. Homosexual attacks and toilet noises add to the chaos. A single cell block in American prisons typically houses several hundred men, sometimes a thousand or more, so that there can be no peace and quiet. Immersed in mass numbers every hour of the day and night, personalities are subject to constant erosion, rumors, fears, and anxieties. One result can be disturbances and riots which draw off some of the frustrations.

Swedish prisons are so great a contrast to American prisons that a visitor finds it hard to realize he is visiting prisons. Langholmen in Stockholm, an old prison and soon to be abandoned, has places for 600 prisoners. This is much too large by Swedish standards. The next largest are Hall and Kumla, each with spaces for about 400. Four other prisons have about 200 each. Some of the larger prisons are central prisons within a district. With six prisons well above the average size of 60, there are other prisons which are well below the average; 17 prisons have less than 30 places.

The Small-group Principle

Swedish prison administrators emphasize the importance of working with prisoners in small groups. The small-group principle is adhered to even when a prison houses several hundred persons. At Kumla, for example, the maximum number of men working in a shop is 30, with most shops having no more than 20. It is possible, in fact, for an inmate, if he so desires, to work in isolation on such materials as leather and jewelry.

Men do not all come together in the same yards. Housing and eating are in groups not larger than 20. In many prisons 10 or 12 in a group is the limit. There are no cells with iron bars; each man has his own room with a wooden door affording complete privacy. Mass anonymity is avoided.

Inmates quite typically carry the keys to their own rooms and come and go with considerable freedom. About one-third of the inmate population is in "open prisons" where an inmate may leave his room at any hour of the day and night and walk out of the building and away from the grounds. (When he does thus escape, he is placed in a more secure place when again apprehended.) Every prison seems to abound with cozy nooks supplied with reading materials, games, and coffee-making equipment, affording opportunities for informal visits and pastimes.

The small-group principle facilitates visiting without clamor not only among inmates but also with staff. Many staff members appear to have a camaraderie type of relationship with the inmates. Large American prisons, on the other hand, tend to provoke fear, in both inmates and staff, resulting in unbridgeable social chasms. It is rare, for example, for a warden to mingle with inmates openly in yard, workshop, or dining hall.

Organization of Prisons

There is a prison for women with about 100 places which serves the entire nation. Also organized on a national basis is a group of institutions which serve young male offenders mostly of the 18-to-21 age category and the institutions for "internees," prisoners who have committed several crimes and whose "mental condition, conduct and other circumstances [necessitates a] long-lasting deprivation of liberty without duration fixed in advance." There is a central prison in each of the last two categories where offenders of these types (youths and internees) are sent by the courts and from which, after a few weeks, they are sorted out to go to specific institutions.

Sweden is divided into five regions for ordinary male adult offenders. Each region has a head prison from which dispersals are made to other institutions within the region.

The courts send convicted offenders to the head institutions; the courts do not determine the specific institutions where offenders will serve their sentences, nor do they dictate the nature of the treatment and training which offenders shall receive.

Within each of the five regions, and within the nation as a whole for youths and internees, there are institutions with different security conditions and a variety of training, treatment, and educational programs.

The regional grouping of prisons facilitates administration. More important, it makes available a variety of institutions to fit the specific needs of prisoners in places not far from their home areas. The inmate's community identification is kept alive through visiting and furlough contacts with family and neighbors. Institutions thus can reflect the local needs, opportunities, and environment in which the offender has his social roots.

Probation and parole are structurally tied to the correctional system, facilitating over-all planning for individual offenders. Some specific prisons are centers to which probationers may be committed for one to two months as part of the probation treatment. In the case of parole some prisons function as halfway houses where prisoners stay at night and on week ends while they work at regular jobs in the community. The parole staff is expected to coordinate training inside and outside the institutions. This makes for continuity in the treatment programs.

Prison Industry and Vocational Training

Anyone informed about American prisons know that idleness is a serious problem. American prison industries which sell goods on the open market are rare. There are more industries which produce goods or services for the prison itself and sometimes for a few other public institutions. A certain amount of inmate labor goes into maintenance of the buildings and grounds and into such services as the procurement, storage and preparation of food for inmates and staff. In addition, some American prisoners have hobby shops where inmates may produce items for themselves and sometimes for sale. Even so, in the average American prison the inmates are kept busy no more than a few hours a day. There are many work projects where several men work at a job which one man could easily do. The general consequence is that men loaf at their work and spend a large amount of their time in the yards and in their cells.

The survey "Correction in the United States" for the President's Commission summarizes the prison work situation in the United States as follows:

> Although the reaction to prison labor restrictions in many states has been constructive and imaginative, taking such forms as work-release programs and a marked increase in the number of conservation and farming activities, the problems of idleness— the meaningless work assignments, the swollen maintenance crews, etc.—remain perplexing concerns of correctional management. The task of motivating the inmate to choose work rather than the alternative—the "idle list" or the isolation cell—is equally perplexing.[9]

The biggest reason for idleness in American correctional institutions is opposition from manufacturers and trade unions. They have been instrumental in the passage of state and federal laws which forbid or restrict various types of work in prisons which might compete with labor and industry on the outside.

In Sweden, on the other hand, all able-bodied prisoners work 42½ hours a week. There are no make-work projects; labor produces goods which are sold on the open market with the explicit approval of labor unions and employer organizations.

Prison shops currently follow four main lines of production: engineering (32 shops with 750 jobs), wood industry (40 shops with 1,132 jobs), mixed industry, including garment manufacture and production of craft goods (81 shops with 2,043 jobs), and building industry (3 shops with 71 jobs). In addition, 1,091 are employed in agricultural and forestry occupations.[10]

Swedish inmates receive wages, though generally at a much lower rate than workers on the outside. Weekly pay for the average prison worker is about eight to ten dollars a week. A piece rate is used wherever possible, even as in Swedish industry generally. Wages are paid not only for regular work hours but also for hours spent in classes relating to the scientific understandings necessary to an occupation, as in electronics. Several institutions are experimenting with pay scales equivalent to those received by workers doing the same work on the outside. The workers then pay for their room and board.

The National Council on Crime and Delinquency reports that in the United States

> Federal Prison Industries, Inc., a creation of the Federal Bureau of Prisons, pays wages ranging from $10 to $75 per month; the average in 1960 was $31.36. The states are generally less generous. A 1957 study in 33 states reported a daily rate of payment ranging from $.04 to $1.30; the average was $.34 a day. At least 10 states provide reduction in sentence as a form of payment for work.[11]

Obviously American prisons make little use of the pay-for-work kind of motivation.

The production equipment in Swedish prisons always seems to be the best and latest available. I was surprised at the large intricate lathes and other machine tools even when such were used only for vocational training. Sweden seems to spare no expense in equipping its industrial-work and vocational-training facilities. Equipment in other parts of the prisons, as in the kitchens and hospitals, is equally impressive.

Security

It is sometimes said that in the United States a man is a good warden to the extent that he can prevent escapes. This negative emphasis is not so great as it once was. However, in conducting a visitor around a prison, an administrator is still likely to point with pride to the facilities which keep men in—the bars which cannot be sawed because of the rolling rods within, the cell-locking system, the armed guards on the walls, and the latest electronic surveillance of all inmate activities.

The stone, cement, high walls, and bars of most American prisons are pervaded by a grim, depressing atmosphere.

About one-third of the prisoners in Sweden are in "open" prisons. Two institutions, Vångdalen and Åby, may serve as examples. Vångdalen is an open prison for youth (age 18-21) located in a wooded and hilly area away from the main roads. It has a capacity of 30, but on the day of my visit only 18 youths were there. Each youth has a separate room, to which he carries his own key. The room is spacious and attractively decorated with colorful drapes, carpeting, chairs, desk, and bedspread. It has solid wooden doors rather than iron bars. It has a radio speaker on which four channels may be selected. The atmosphere is informal.

In the shops the boys were producing bed frames and other furniture items. One boy was whistling while working at his job. This did not mean that the job was highly desirable or that all the boys were happy. But it surely was the first inmate I have ever heard whistling at his job in all my prison visits in the United States, Mexico, and England.

The boys are allowed freedom on the grounds, and in fact they have the freedom to walk away from the institution at almost any hour of day or night. There is no wall, not even a fence. There are only small signs indicating the limits of the institution's grounds. Boys can escape with ease, and a sizable number do walk away. They are readily apprehended and then go into a more secure institution.

I raised the question with the prison governor whether it would not be well to have a high fence some distance out from the buildings, a fence which would not prevent all escapes but which might make a youth think twice before trying to escape. Extreme permissiveness and ease of escape would seem to place too great a strain on a youth's self-control, a personal quality in which he might be lacking and a basic reason why he was there. "After all," I said, "we do many things, such as locking our cars, proctoring examinations in school, and policing our highways to frustrate 'good people' from getting into trouble." But the governor insisted that the individual must learn to control himself and not to depend on control provided by the environment. "Until he learns 'inner control,' mastering his impulses in a highly permissive environment, and until he learns how to use his time in a positive manner without outward coercion and restraint, he cannot become a good community citizen."

I raised the same question in several other institutions, but the answers were always the same.

Åby is an open prison for male adults. It has spaces for 52 inmates. This prison has more of the "harder criminals" than any other open prison. The inmates work in a wood-industry shop and on 1,200 acres of farm and timber land. Again the rooms, dining areas, nooks, and the like are conducive to a homelike atmosphere. There are private rooms rather than cells.

There is no fence or wall. It is easy to walk away, and the governor admitted that many escape, though they are readily apprehended and are then placed in a more secure institution. Presumably those who stand the test of freedom without infringing on it can return to their communities with stronger "inner controls," such as ultrasecurity institutions cannot produce.

With a few exceptions, the "closed prisons" in Sweden are not of a high security type by American standards. Only a few have walls; most have common fences some little distance from the shops and living quarters. Two institutions, Hall and Kumla, may serve as examples of the closed type.

The Hall Prison is the central institution for the security (recidivist) group. It has capacity for 300 inmates, and about 2,000 acres of land. Seventy of the 300 places are in open cottages with no fences or guards and where each man carries the key to his own room. The rest of the institution is "closed" and has a wall. There are no armed guards here or in any other Swedish prison. What fascinated me was the free and easy way Gunnar Marnell, general director of all the security institutions, moved among the inmates on a first-name basis. "Prisoners are people," he said, "people who are temporarily in prison. They must be treated as citizens, not as a permanent convict class."

Kumla is a security prison and the central institution for the Inland area. It is new. Its emphasis on ultrasecurity is puzzling, since it receives the regular run of court cases for its region most of whom are here for only a few weeks before they are dispersed to the special institutions of the Inland group. It is inconsistent with the architecture of other prisons. It has high walls and locked doors. It has electronic surveillance of inmates at all times. The Swedish government had planned a central institution of the Kumla type for each of the five regional groups of prisons. However, the building of Kumla raised a great public protest throughout Sweden—so much so that plans for the building of more such prisons have been scrapped.

Even at Kumla, however, as pointed out above, the small-group principle and individual rooms prevail, so that in spite of the security provisions there is a much more informal and relaxed atmosphere than prevails in the average American prison.

Respect for the Individual

Retaliation and vengeance against offenders plays little or no part in the Swedish correctional system. To those who insist on punishment, the usual reply of prison administrators in Sweden is that the loss of freedom is punishment enough. A spirit of enlightened humaneness characterizes the treatment of offenders. Norval Morris, professor of law and criminology and director of the Center for Studies in Criminal Justice, University of Chicago, thinks that the Swedish social and political system is pervaded by

> . . . a high level of respect for individual human rights. . . . [Sweden] is . . . a very polite society in which citizen treats citizen and the state treats its citizens with punctilious respect. These attitudes lie deep in Swedish social organization and are in no way abandoned when the citizen becomes a criminal or a prisoner. . . .
>
> This humanitarian and egalitarian attitude is indeed the mainspring of the whole correctional system, an explanation of both the low incidence of imprisonment and of many of the conditions and practices within the prison system.
>
> [The average Swedish citizen insists that] the Swedish criminal or prisoner still remains a Swedish citizen meriting respect, continuing properly to enjoy a quite high standard of living and remaining a part of the community. These sentiments are brought to his work by the prison officer who sees a Swedish quality of firm, decent, respectful, and polite treatment between individuals

as properly determining his attitude and behavior towards the inmate. It is a great asset, substantially diminishing the alienating prison subculture creating processes that are to be found so often in other countries.[12]

The Swedish respect for personal rights which do not infringe on the rights of others was illustrated in the first youth prison I visited. After a general tour I commented on the long, curly hair of some of the inmates, and I asked if having long hair was ever interpreted as a symbol of non-conformity and rebellion, since this seems to be its meaning in the United States. The staff was surprised when I said that there are some institutions, even some public schools, which require boys to cut their long hair. The prison governor stated that the length of an individual's hair is a personal matter and no one should be required to change it. Along a similar vein he stated that every Sunday the boys are allowed visitors in their private rooms, including girl friends even if this means that sex relations take place. He said that such relations are personal and private matters about which the prison staff does not concern itself.

In keeping with the spirit of respect for persons, the convicted offender who is not considered dangerous is often asked to deliver himself to a certain prison by a certain date. If he must be conveyed there by authority, *The Law on Treatment in Correctional Institutions in Sweden* states that "all possible care shall be taken not to expose him to the undue attention of people. If he has fetters, they shall be hidden under his clothing."

Perhaps the general sentiment of the public can be gauged in part by the development of a citizens' organization which, far from decrying the general permissiveness in prisons or condemning them as country clubs, criticizes the prison administration for not being permissive enough. I had an interview with Jorgen Erickson, one of the editors of *Dagens Nyheter,* the largest daily newspaper in Sweden. Erickson was one of the founders of the KRUM organization, the letters of which stand for the Swedish version of "Organization for Humanization of Treatment of Criminals." The organization was begun in 1966 and now has 7,500 members, about half of whom are former inmates. KRUM now also exists in Finland, Norway, and Denmark. This Scandinavian organization is the only one of its kind in the world. Erickson said:

> . . . prisoners must have a chance to speak for themselves. People in schools, and in other public and private organizations, generally have ample opportunity to disseminate their points of view concerning their respective rights. But prisoners and former inmates are almost totally lacking in such opportunities. They need a chance to make known their attitudes concerning prisons and other penal sanctions.

KRUM also tries to help former inmates get jobs as they come out of prison or perhaps before they are released. The members of KRUM visit inmates in prisons and seek to render aid on personal and legal problems of a kind which persons officially connected with the prison would find it hard to give. We seek the right to visit inmates without supervision by prison personnel and without the necessity of working through the prison hierarchy.

KRUM members make many talks concerning prisons before clubs and groups of various kinds. Frequently such presentations are made in pairs of one inmate and one non-inmate.

Since many inmates come from the lower social classes, and since many non-inmate members of KRUM are professional and business persons, KRUM provides an avenue of communication between two segments of the population which often have difficulty understanding each other.

KRUM is pushing for more pay for inmates in industrial-type work and for more emphasis on treatment and education. The institutions need more psychologists and psychiatrists to implement their programs in the most effective manner.

One of the chief concerns of KRUM in the last few years is that there be no more building of prisons such as Kumla. The government had planned to build five such prisons, one for each of the regional districts. Due to our opposition, and the critical reactions from the general public, we are confident that no more prisons like Kumla will be erected.

The ultimate hope of KRUM is that, except for dangerous persons, prisons be abolished altogether. We think society would be better off without them.

The Prisoner and the Outside World

One of the professed goals of prisons in modern societies is the rehabilitation of persons who have committed crimes. Such persons are presumably discordant with society as a whole and especially with their families and local communities. However, the dilemma is that a prison term extracts the individual from his social setting. If he is to be resocialized so that he can become once again a respected citizen and a good family man, how can this be done by taking him out of his community? When he is out of sight, he is also likely to be out of mind, so that his community may forget him and his family may break up. The offender himself is generally in no position to improve his social skills while he is in prison.

There is probably no real solution for this dilemma. However, the problem can be ameliorated if the community, through frequent contacts with the prisoner, is kept aware that he is still their responsibility. Resocialization should be easier if it is possible to make frequent visits with him in prison and if the prisoner has furlough leaves to be at home a few days now and then. It helps if the prison is fairly near the home environment. It is also advantageous if the prisoner's earning power is not impaired, so his family will not be disgraced by having to go on relief.

Visiting privileges are liberal in the prisons of Sweden. In most prisons relatives are allowed to visit inmates every Sunday. Many Swedish prisons permit visitors, including wives or girl friends, to visit inmates in the privacy of their rooms. In addition to their private rooms there are small nooks and spaces for visiting and drinking coffee. The small, informal Swedish prisons make visiting easy and pleasant.

In 1937 Sweden passed a limited-furlough law enabling a prisoner to receive leaves for a fixed period of time "to visit a relative who is seriously ill or to attend the funeral of a relative." Furloughs of this type were approved only in exceptional cases where the risk could be regarded as non-existent. Only the National Correctional Administration could approve specific furloughs.

Since the initial experience with furloughs was good, the system has been greatly expanded. Special circumstances warrant special furloughs. Since 1963 such furloughs are granted not only for cases of illness or death but also for the chance "to appear as a witness in a court of law, to confer with a prospective employer, landlord or other persons in order to obtain employment or living quarters after discharge or parole."[13]

Regular furloughs, without special circumstances, are also available to the great majority of prisoners. Prisoners who are sentenced for 10 months or more in "open institutions" receive their first regular furlough after 6 months and every 3 months thereafter. A prisoner serving 18 months or more in a "closed institution" is eligible for a furlough at the end of 10 months and every 4 months thereafter. The first furlough is normally for 48 hours plus travel time, and succeeding furloughs are for 72 hours plus travel time. Furloughs are not granted to men considered dangerous.

Prison directors in Sweden consider the furlough system a success. The ten prison governors with whom I discussed the system agreed that it helps to keep alive a prisoner's interest in his family and community. It reminds people in the community that the inmate is still a part of them and that sometime he will return permanently. Furloughs enable the prisoner to make plans for the future, including employment and housing. Several governors stated that furloughs help reduce sex tensions in prisons. Swedish prisons are apparently quite free of homosexuality.

Rather than restrict or abolish furloughs, there are some Swedish prison authorities who think they should be expanded, particularly for those prisoners who are nearing their time of release. Some think there should be experimentation with longer furloughs, such as 30-day leaves.

Furloughs for American prisoners are relatively rare and are restricted almost entirely to cases of death or serious illness in the family.

Prison Staff

No prison system is better than its staff. The finest equipment, the best standards, and the most suitable architectural settings fail if the personnel are not suited by training and temperament for the jobs.

In his article in *Federal Probation,* Morris states that the emphasis on humanitarian and human rights in Swedish prisons is a source of strength and that it is also a source of weakness so far as the staff is concerned, for

> . . . staff training is far from well-developed and that which exists is at a low level of technical sophistication, reliance being placed very heavily on the personality and decency of the staff member with insufficient attention being given to his training.[14]

However, Swedish prison administrators are not in their positions by reason of political patronage. No one reaches the top administrative levels without a variety of work experiences within the correctional system.

Since Morris wrote his article, Sweden's legislature, in 1966, has provided the legal basis and finances for an ambitious staff-training program. The projected basic training comprises a year of theoretical courses combined with practical work. This program includes three phases: (1) Orientation. This takes place in the institution to which the employee is assigned. It involves instruction in rules and regulations and practical training under the supervision of experienced staff. (2) In-service training. After about three months of training the new employee who appears to be suited to the work attends a 5-week in-service course. (3) Coordinated training. After one year the employee who appears to be suited to correctional work is expected to enroll in a 12-week series of courses in such fields as psychology, social science, and jurisprudence centrally administered by the Welfare Training Board.

Sweden employs a number of women in practically all prisons, not only in secretarial work in the front offices but also within the workshops and housing and eating areas. In fact, a few institutions for male offenders have women governors. Two of eight regional directors of prisons are woman. General Director of Prisons Torsten Ericksson told me that within the present decade "women governors will take over one prison after another. It is my impression that they are as good disciplinarians as men. Women employees generally add a softening influence to prison life and produce a more normal society."

In recent years there have been more jobs in the Swedish economy than manpower available. This is reflected in the prisons, especially in the case of professional persons, such as doctors, psychiatrists, psychologists, and sociologists. A number of prison governors complained that although they are equipped for professional staff, they have been unable to obtain sufficient help of this kind. Some stated there is a larger turnover of general prison personnel than they consider desirable.

With few exceptions state prisons in the United States employ relatively few well-trained employees. They lack budgets large enough to draw such persons. Many employees do not find the grim prisons with large convict populations to be desirable places to work. Perhaps some of the public stigma stamped on convicts carries over to some of the employees also. The few highly qualified staff members of such institutions often are frustrated because their programs cannot be implemented by employees who are without training and without understanding of the professional goals and techniques.

The President's Commission Survey of Correction in the United States summarizes the staff situation in United States prisons as follows:

> . . . [13 states] have a ratio of professional staff members (psychiatrists, psychologists, social workers and counselors) to inmates of less than 1:100. One state has a ratio of 1:55; on the other hand, 11 states have professional staff-inmate ratios not better than 1:500. The national average is 1:179.
>
> Many more persons are employed in custodial than in treatment positions. The average officer-inmate ratio for the nation is 1:7, with a range from 1:3 in a New England state, to 1:200 in a state using armed guards.
>
> The ratio of all employees to inmates averages 1:4; it ranges from 1:2 to 1:59. . . .
>
> Standards call for merit system coverage for all institutional employees. . . . In practice, civil service does not apply to superintendents in 54 per cent of the states, to professional employees in 28 per cent, and to custodial officers in 26 per cent. . . . A

merit system for institutional employees does not exist in 13 states. . . .

Only 24 per cent of all jurisdictions require the [prison] superintendent to have a college degree; 48 per cent have no minimum educational requirements whatever. . . . In three states an applicant who could not qualify for the guard position because he lacked a high school diploma would not be disqualified for the superintendency.

Qualifications for the professional positions vary, and the meaning of the position title itself is not uniform throughout the states. In 28 per cent of all jurisdictions, one can be a "professional worker" without having graduated from high school. In at least one jurisdiction the mail clerk is called a "social worker."[15]

Parole and Probation

A well-adjusted prisoner in Sweden may be released when he has served from one-half to two-thirds of his sentence. Release before the end of a term places the individual under supervision subject to the possibility that he may be returned to the institution if he behaves badly under parole.

The Swedish *Penal Code* provides for probation, not as a conditional suspension of sentence but as a supervised period. During this time the probation order may be revoked and some other sanction imposed if the rules for conduct are broken. The law also provides that the court may commit the probationer to an institution "for a period of not less than one and not more than two months." This is defined as part of the treatment of probation and may be necessary to remove the probationer from an undesirable milieu or to extricate him from alcoholism. The correctional institutions for probationers are always special, small, and open.

There is a trend in Sweden toward placing a larger percentage of offenders under probationary supervision rather than in prisons. Whereas the number of individuals sentenced to prisons during the past ten years has remained more or less constant, the number of persons placed on probation increased from 3,847 in 1956 to 7,884 in 1967, or by 60 per cent.[16] Similar trends are evident in the United States

Sweden makes extensive use of voluntary supervisors for probationers and parolees, as do some other European countries. Presently there are over 10,000 such supervisors in Sweden, each supervising one to three cases. The supervisors are supported by some 47 community boards, each under the chairmanship of a judge or a lawyer. Such boards have the power to lay down the conditions for probation and parole and to terminate or extend the periods of supervisory care. Between the boards and the volunteers is a staff of 150 professional consultants who advise and assist the volunteers.

Morris says of this system that it

. . . has the advantage of mobilizing the interest of many thoughtful people throughout Sweden as supervisors. The program brings them deeply into the total correctional system. . . . It tends also to maximize the local community's interest in and support for the probationer and ex-prisoner. Some of the supervisors are professionally trained in the social sciences; many are school teachers. . . . [The system's] main disadvantage is one that permeates corrections in Sweden—it provides little technically skilled social casework assistance to the offender, and there are certainly cases where such is needed.[17]

EVALUATION OF THE SWEDISH CORRECTIONAL SYSTEM

In many respects the Swedish correctional system is probably the most advanced in the world. It meets many of the specifications for prison reform which the United States Federal Bureau of Prisons has been advocating for years. Swedish prisons are small and specialized for different types of treatment and individuals. At the same time they receive the benefits of a larger system of administration and facilities. Sentences are usually short, with the realization that long terms produce institutionalized personalities which cannot function outside of prison. Most prisons have minimum security, so that the grim repressiveness of bars, cells, and high walls is experienced by relatively few prisoners. Liberal visiting privileges in homelike living quarters are permitted. The law provides that each inmate can have furnishings in his room similar to those at home. Furlough privileges break the institutional routines and help preserve family and community ties. The curse of idleness does not exist; every able-bodied man works 42½ hours a week at useful industrial and agricultural production. It is almost impossible to imagine a more humane correctional system; from it vengeance and retaliation have been removed.

One of the complaints heard most often from prison administrators was that they found it difficult to attract sufficient professional personnel, particularly psychiatrists, sociologists, and psychologists. The smallness and the scatter of the institutions often make it necessary to share experts between several institutions. This, plus the fact that such personnel are in short supply in Sweden, and the fact that private types of employment may be more remunerative, helps to account for the difficulty. In time this shortage of professional personnel may be cleared, when the government realizes it is quite as important to provide expert manpower as it is to provide the latest technological equipment.

A number of prison administrators stated that the program dealing with work was theoretical and involved vocational training as well as actual engagement in productive work. The evidence for productive work is abundant. Large well-lit and well-equipped shops hum with activity, with most prisoners earning on a piecework basis. Except for some handicapped prisoners in hobby shops, there are obviously no make-work products and there is no loafing on the job.

However, the evidence for theoretical and vocational training is scant. Much of the productive work is repetitive, quite generally a matter of cutting or shaping a large number of identical pieces of wood or metal. Such work scarcely adds up to any particular skill unless just the ability to stick to a repetitive job is thought of as a skill. Vocational training, involving the theory and nature of materials and designs, seems to be largely lacking. As in the United States, many of the inmates are from lower-income classes who are handicapped educationally, and since industrial progress creates constant demands for new skills and more trained manpower, it would seem that vocational training should be of some importance. Although I was excited about the busy work in Swedish prisons in contrast to the vast amount of idleness and make-work in American prisons, I could not see much evidence that an inmate might learn the skills required of a plumber, a carpenter, a printer, or an automobile mechanic. If an inmate comes out of prison without gaining much of a change in his skills, the chances would seem to be great that he will fit once more into the same or similar work environment with the same human associations which originally might have been a factor leading him into crime. One reason for the difficulty of training workers in skills is that two-thirds of all prisoners spend less than four months at an institution. Prison and parole authorities generally try to place inmates in job-learning situations upon release.

The final test of a prison system based on the principle of rehabilitation is how many individuals are really reconditioned in such a way that they will not get into serious trouble again. The question can be posed, but it is difficult to answer.

Swedish prisons have data regarding the number of parolees who break parole regulations. Several prison wardens stated that about 75 per cent of the offenders let out on parole break regulations and thus spend more time in prison. How many break parole regulations is not a valid measure, however, of the effectiveness of prisons. A parolee in Sweden, as well as in the United States, is subject to a variety of rules concerning his activities and behavior in addition to the regular criminal code. The nature of such rules and the manner in which violations are handled differ considerably from one time to another and even more from one country to another. In Sweden some violations are interpreted as petty and frequently mean that the offender is remanded to prison again for only a short stay of a few weeks. Many such petty violations could be overlooked altogether, and the record would show up quite differently. In any case recidivism because of parole violations is not a valid index of the relative effectiveness of the rehabilitation programs in prisons.

The recidivism rate for American ex-convicts is generally considered to be at least 50 per cent. Swedish prison authorities estimate the repeater rate of Swedish prisoners at 15 per cent.

72 Deviant Behavior in Sweden

While they cannot supply exact figures, they think this percentage is close to the truth.

In 1967, 116 persons were sentenced to "internment," an indefinite length of sentence for persons who have been sentenced on two or more occasions in the past. The total thus sentenced in 1967 constituted about 1 per cent of all persons sentenced to prison in 1967.[18] Apparently the prison system does rehabilitate the great majority of inmates—or the inmates rehabilitate themselves in spite of the prison experience.

There is no way of knowing with any certainty, but it may be that modern societies, except for a few offenders who are dangerous, could do without prisons altogether. It may be, as the Swedish KRUM organization maintains, that society would not have more crime, and would perhaps have even less, if prisons did not exist. It is evident that many criminologists have less faith in the prison system than was held some decades ago and that courts are applying more and more non-institutional sanctions.

However, if it is assumed that societies must have prisons, then it would seem that the Swedish system is built on sounder sociological principles than most other prison systems, including that of the United States. If rehabilitation is the goal, short sentences generally make more sense than long years of imprisonment—years which are bound to stultify and institutionalize the human personality so that it can never really function in freedom again. Likewise, from what we know of groups and crowds, small prisons have a better chance of preserving individuality and avoiding the erosion of personality resulting from lack of privacy and constant exposure to a mass environment. Furloughs and a liberal visiting policy help to preserve family ties. Useful work with pay helps to preserve self-respect and prevents demoralization.

It is quite certain that the Swedish system of corrections does not leave inmates thoroughly resentful, as the American system so generally does. Convicts in American prisons are easily embittered by the grim repressive environment—the steel bars, the high walls, the utter lack of privacy. Bitterness also results from the typical attitude of the American public toward the man who has been in prison—the "ex-con"—who is feared and stigmatized, not so much because he has committed crimes but because he has been in prison, where, the chances are, he has learned much about crime and criminals. The prototype of the public's attitude in the United States is represented by the local police, who generally suspect and check likely ex-convicts in the community when crimes have been committed.

As with most generalizations, there are exceptions. There are men who have served sentences in American prisons who make good and who eventually, if not immediately, receive the public's respect. Such persons, however, generally make good in spite of the prison experience rather than because of it.

There is much that can be learned about the rehabilitation process from the Swedish correctional system. It should be added that the prison system is a creation of the Swedish welfare state within the last few decades, a creation designed not to punish but to change attitudes.

NOTES

1. *The Penal Code of Sweden* has been translated into English by Thorsten Sellin, professor of sociology, University of Pennsylvania, with an Introduction by Ivar Strahl, professor of criminal law, University of Uppsala.
2. Edwin H. Sutherland & Donald R. Cressey, *Principles of Criminology* (Philadelphia: Lippincott, 1966), pp. 437 f.
3. *Crime in America: The Challenge of Crime in a Free Society*, Report by the President's Commission on Law Enforcement and Administration of Justice (Washington: Govt. Printing Office, 1967), pp. 25-29.
4. FBI, *Uniform Crime Reports, 1968*, Table 16 (p. 109).
5. Edwin H. Sutherland, *The Professional Thief: By a Professional Thief* (Chicago: Univ. of Chicago Press, 1967).
6. A few of the best-known studies include William Isaac Thomas & Florian Znaniecki, *The Polish Peasant in Europe and America* (New York: Knopf, 1927); Lewis Yablonsky, *The Violent Gang* (New York: Pelican, 1966); Richard A. Cloward & Lloyd E. Ohlin, *Delinquency and Opportunity* (Glencoe, Ill.: Free Press, 1960); Malcolm W. Klein, *Juvenile Gangs in Context* (Englewood Cliffs, N.J.: Prentice-Hall, 1967).
7. Albert Cohen, *Boy Delinquents: The Culture of the Delinquent Gang* (Glencoe, Ill.: Free Press, 1955), pp. 36-44.
8. FBI, *Uniform Crime Reports, 1967*, p. 1.

9. "Correction in the United States: A Survey for the President's Commission," *Crime and Delinquency,* Vol. 13, No. 1 (Jan., 1967), p. 200.

10. *Kriminalvarden 1966* (Stockholm: Kriminalvardsstyrelsen, 1967), pp. 14 f.

11. "Correction in the United States . . . ," *ibid.*

12. "Lessons From the Adult Correctional System of Sweden," *Federal Probation,* Vol. 30 (Dec., 1966), p. 5. Quoted by permission of the author.

13. Torsten Ericksson, Director General of the Swedish Correctional System, "The Swedish Furlough System for Prisoners." Unpublished paper.

14. "Lessons from the Adult Correctional System . . . ," *ibid.* Used by permission of the author.

15. "Correction in the United States . . . ," *ibid.,* pp. 194 f.

16. *Statistical Abstract of Sweden, 1968,* Table 335 (p. 310).

17. "Lessons From the Adult Correctional System . . . ,"*ibid.,* p. 12. Used by permission of the author.

18. *Kriminalvarden 1967* (Stockholm: Sveriges Officiella Statistik. 1968).

IV

Alcoholism

*Ode to the Potato**

In this, our cold and barren land,
No ripened grapes are near at hand;
But deep in the ground
The "Northern Grapes" are found,
Whose juice stimulates us with a fiery glow,
As drink we down—all at one go.

The Scandinavian countries have long drinking histories from the days of the Vikings. But it was aquavit, the potato alcohol, which sent the Scandinavians on a prolonged bender. The "consumption of aquavit," says Dahlberg, "reached a very high level during the eighteenth and beginning of the nineteenth centuries. The Swedish people were a drunken people, at least during the afternoons."[1]

Although Swedish soil and climate are not suitable for most vegetables, potatoes can be raised in abundance. They became very popular not only as a food but also as an inexpensive source of alcohol. The production of aquavit was simple. Thousands of peasants distilled their own potato spirits just as they produced wheat for their bread. What Christie has recently written about Norway could no doubt also be said about Sweden: "In 1815 all Norwegian landowners . . . were given the right to distill liquor and most took broad advantage of it. . . . Observers described Norway as a thoroughly alcoholized country."[2]

A temperance movement beginning in the early 19th century resulted in restrictive legislation by the middle of the century. It sought to abolish the household distilleries and to control the

---

*Free translation of a Swedish drinking song.

wholesale and retail sales of alcoholic beverages through local and national regulations. The right to sell potato spirits was limited by special detailed regulations. The right to monopolize local retail trade in the towns was given to certain companies controlled by the government. These companies could close the saloons and turn them into restaurants where limited amounts of potato spirits could be served with meals. The temperance movement at this time was concerned only with potato alcohol. In time, when the public began to demand other strong liquors, there began a search for more drastic controls.

FORTY YEARS OF RATIONING

In the early years of the 20th century there was considerable sentiment favorable to national prohibition. Organized labor was particularly concerned about straightening out the drinking problems of some of its members. The longshoremen in Stockholm were a case in point. They were poorly paid and earned the nickname of "harbor bums." Employers complained about the drinking and yet allowed the workers to eat and drink in waterfront inns where the wages were paid, sometimes barely enough to cover the bills. Union leaders got the city to close the waterfront inns, and the longshoremen were eventually more or less straightened out. In 1909 there was a six-week general strike in Sweden during which the government was able to prohibit the sale of spirits. This led to further experiments with governmental controls.

Public sentiment for prohibition was running high. Prohibition was not, however, put into effect, perhaps mainly because Dr. Ivan Bratt, a physician in Stockholm, was able to convince government officials that total prohibition would not work. Bratt believed that a more feasible solution was to restrict individuals in how much alcohol they could buy, such restriction to be imposed by rationing. In 1917 the Swedish legislature approved the Bratt system, a unique form of handling the traffic in alcohol which was to continue for forty years.

Passbooks were issued only to income earners who were at

least 25 years old. Married women, and women without income, were not eligible for ration books. The size of the rations depended somewhat on personal income and social status. The maximum ration varied between three and four quarts of distilled alcohol a month. The ration books could be withdrawn from persons who failed to pay their taxes on time or who developed a record of getting drunk. Restaurants were allowed to serve a small amount of liquor with meals, so that eating out was a way by which one could supplement one's regular ration. Bars and saloons were forbidden. Wines were not rationed, but purchases were entered on the passbooks. Beer which did not exceed 2.8 per cent alcohol was freely available.

The system seems to have worked tolerably well in the early years, probably far better than would have been possible under a system of prohibition. But in time abuses appeared and increased, until the public demanded an end to rationing. It was said that men who did not drink, or drank very little, would buy the monthly allotments and pass them on to friends. Eating in restaurants increased considerably, often with a waste of food because the real object was the alcohol supplement to the regular ration. Connery describes some other developments:

> Predictably, Swedes took to moonshining, bootlegging and the black marketing of ration books. People in southern Sweden sailed regularly to Copenhagen, where they drank furiously to the amusement and disgust of the Danes. Protests against the Bratt System mounted, and Dr. Bratt himself came under such abuse that he took up residence in France. It appeared that the system, far from curbing drinking, was making it more desirable, especially to the young. An investigation showed that 75 per cent of all the alcohol offenses were committed by persons who had been denied the passbook. The worst of the situation was that a law-abiding nation was breaking the law right and left, and a democratic nation was putting up with a disturbing amount of state control of private behavior.[3]

THE PRESENT STATE SYSTEM OF ALCOHOL CONTROL

Rationing of alcohol was abolished in 1955. The new approach is less restrictive and places more emphasis on positive measures, such as scientific research, and on education with a strong emphasis on individual responsibility. The state, however, retains strict control over the production and the wholesale and retail trade in alcoholic beverages.

High state taxes on liquor are a large part of the temperance policy. In general, the higher the alcohol content of the drink, the higher the tax. The high prices are designed to delimit the use of alcohol and to shift consumption from spirits, with high alcoholic content, to wines and beer. The high prices obviously affect the working people much more than people of wealth. Moreover, the state liquor system is trying to encourage customers to buy more wine by stocking a large variety of wines and more beer by making it available in many restaurants. It is not known whether these policies explain the doubling in the rate of wine and beer consumption since 1955.

The age of eligibility for the purchase of alcohol has been lowered from 25, of the Bratt system, to 21. Alcohol abusers, such as those twice convicted of drunken driving, those convicted of producing alcohol, and those branded as habitual drunks by local temperance boards, are forbidden to buy alcohol. Citizens in good standing may buy as much as they wish.

Only monopolistic liquor stores, over which the government has complete control, sell spirits and wine. Beer can be bought in grocery stores and restaurants. Liquor stores cannot be found in all towns. Some communities, with as many as 30,000 or 40,000 inhabitants, are without such stores because of the strength of the local temperance organization.

Liquor stores are not allowed to advertise. Most stores are unattractive, with almost no liquor on display. Signs display slogans such as "Say No to Liquor." Bottles are kept under the counter and on shelves inaccessible to the purchaser. One can buy only by name or number from a catalogue. Purchases are wrapped in gray-green paper readily identifiable on the street. It is said that many a buyer is embarrassed with his liquor package if observed by acquaintances on his way home. "The temperance movement," says Fleisher "has without question succeeded in filling many Swedes with guilt about drinking."

Licensed restaurants, in principle, still can sell liquor only with food. At present this requirement has been experimentally suspended in large parts of Sweden except where local authorities oppose it. *Akvavik*, generally regarded as the greatest threat to public sobriety, can be served in restaurants only with meals.

RATES OF CONSUMPTION

The average annual consumption of pure alcohol per inhabitant 15 years and over is estimated to have been about 2.1 gallons a century ago. The present figure is 1.7 gallons. (Table 2.) Swedes are drinking more than several decades ago but not significantly more.

TABLE 2

Annual Consumption in Gallons of Pure Alcohol Per Inhabitant 15 Years & Over, Sweden 1861-1968*

Year	Gallon	Year	Gallon	Year	Gallon
1861-65	2.1	1938	1.1	1955	1.4
1866-70	1.9	1939	1.1	1956	1.5
1871-75	2.6	1940	.9	1957	1.4
1876-80	2.3	1941	.8	1958	1.2
1881-85	1.9	1942	.9	1959	1.3
1886-90	1.8	1943	.9	1960	1.3
1891-95	1.8	1944	.9	1961	1.3
1896-00	2.1	1945	1.0	1962	1.3
1901-05	2.0	1946	1.1	1963	1.3
1906-10	1.7	1947	1.2	1964	1.4
1911-15	1.6	1948	1.2	1965	1.5
1916-20	.9	1949	1.2	1966	1.6
1921-25	1.1	1950	1.2	1967	1.7
1926-30	1.1	1951	1.2	1968	1.7
1931-35	1.0	1952	1.3		
1936	1.0	1953	1.3		
1937	1.1	1954	1.3		

* Swedish data for the period 1861-1935 are given only per inhabitant of entire population. On the assumption that children under 15 drink little or no alcoholic beverages, I have computed the amount of consumption per inhabitant 15 years and over, thus making the early period comparable with the period after 1935.

Source: National Board of Excise, Stockholm. (This board is the authority on statistical information on alcohol consumption in Sweden.)

PATTERNS OF DRINKING

As shown in Table 3, convictions for drunkenness increased considerably during the immediate years after rationing was abolished in 1955; there was a relatively large increase in drunkenness, especially in the 15-17 age group. The rate of convictions for drunkenness in the whole population declined, however, after 1956.

TABLE 3

Changes in Convictions for Drunkenness at Various Ages, Sweden 1928-65 (Reckoned per 1,000 inhabitants in each age group; 1928 is given the base level of 100)

Year	Age 15-17	Age 18-20	Age 21-24	The Entire Population Over 15 Years of Age
1928	100	100	100	100
1954	333	207	145	126
1956	700	395	249	260
1958	700	343	207	216
1960	933	372	199	208
1962	1055	412	199	205
1964*	1044	398	200	202
1965*	1111	402	193	205

* Estimated.

Source: Nils Sundberg, "The Alcohol Question in Sweden" (unpublished ms.), p. 5.

Bruun and Hauge made an intensive study in 1963 of the drinking habits of youth in the capital cities of the Scandinavian countries—Helsinki, Stockholm, Oslo, and Copenhagen.[4] The study does not support stories of wild drinking by Scandinavian youth. In Stockholm, 60 per cent of a random sample of 135 14-year-old boys, 83 per cent of 150 16-year-olds, and 87 per cent of 18-year-olds had used alcohol. Although 78 per cent of the 18-year-olds had used spirits, most of the beverages consumed consisted of beer and wine. Although it is widespread, "the drinking is sporadic and the quantity consumed on each occasion is small."[5] According to Bruun and Hauge, nearly all the drinking by

Stockholm youth occurs at home or in restaurants; only 10 per cent occurs "elsewhere." Most drinking is done in the presence of parents or with the knowledge of parents.[6] The study seems at variance with the data of Sundberg above. Sundberg got his data from police arrest records, whereas Bruun and Hauge relied on interviews of youths themselves. However, the data may appear to be more contradictory than they really are. A relatively few hard-drinking youths can send up the arrest rates while the great majority may be drinking moderately.

Sweden continues to have a strong preoccupation with the personal and social problems of the use of alcohol even though the average consumption of distilled liquor is much less than in past centuries and drinking has become more controlled.

There is a marked difference in drinking habits between the sexes. Swedish women drink considerably less than Swedish men, and there are few female heavy drinkers. Only about 3 per cent of the total number of cases of drunkenness are accounted for by women. As has been said about women drinkers in the United States, "they typically learn a drinking style that goes along with being female."[7]

For every hundred male alcoholics in Sweden there are only three or four female alcoholics. In the United States the ratio of female alcoholics to male alcoholics is higher, with about 20 women to every 100 men. The most marked development in Sweden in recent years is that drinking habits begin earlier in life for both sexes, and the amount of drunkenness among young people has increased.[8]

A comparison between countries regarding alcohol consumption per capita says nothing about the differences in the patterns of drinking. In some countries, such as Italy, many people drink regularly and moderately, while in other countries, such as Finland, fewer people drink, but they drink irregularly and immoderately. Sweden's per capita consumption rates are relatively moderate, but Sweden still has problems with alcohol abuse. Although there are apparently fewer drunks and fewer alcoholics than fifty or a hundred years ago, in some respects the drinking is more problematic since it takes place in a technological age where personal self-control is of significance for the economy.

Table 4, compiled by V. Efron and M. Keller, gives us information about the patterns of drinking in terms of different beverages.

TABLE 4

Apparent Consumption of Distilled Spirits, Wine & Beer in Certain Countries, in Liters per Capita of the Population Aged 15 Years & Over (Last Available Year in Each Country)

Country	Year	Spirits		Wine		Beer		Total
		Bev.	Absolute Alcohol	Bev.	Absolute Alcohol	Bev.	Absolute Alcohol	Absolute Alcohol
France	1955	6.29†	3.15	191.96	20.16	77.27*	3.37	26.68
Italy	1960	2.70†	1.35	144.73	11.57	7.70	0.34	13.26
Switzerland	1950-55	3.93	1.57	44.37	4.66	98.68*	4.62	10.85
Germany (W)	1960	6.42†	2.44	10.9**	1.09**	120.72	5.31	8.84
U.S.A.	1962	7.53	3.41	5.00	0.83	83.19	3.75	7.99
Canada	1961	5.60†	2.24	3.19	0.51	89.60	4.48	7.23
United Kingdom	1960	1.70	0.97	1.4**	0.24**	110.08	4.95	6.16
Denmark	1959	1.68	0.84	3.93	0.63	93.18	4.10	5.57
Sweden	1959	6.17	3.15	4.07	0.52	37.27	1.31	4.98
Germany (E)	1960	5.37†	1.88	4.00	0.40	89.40	2.68	4.60
Ireland	1959	1.74	0.99	1.19	0.20	65.74	2.96	4.15
Norway	1960	3.95	1.71	1.68	0.25	33.19	1.49	3.45
Finland	1960	4.91	2.46	1.84	0.39	1.06	0.48	3.33

(*) Includes "cider"
(**) Values for wine extrapolated from earlier reports.
(†) Values converted from original reports in terms of absolute alcohol.

Notes:
The alcohol content of beverages varies among countries. Calculations for this table are based on the best available information from each country.

Only countries from which adequate statistics on both alcohol and population, not more than 10 years old, are available, have been included in this tabulation.

Compiled by V. Efron and M. Keeler of the staff of Ruger's University Center of Alcohol Studies.

Alcoholism

There is much ambiguity about what can be considered a "proper use of alcohol" in Sweden even as in the United States. A major source of this ambiguity lies in the historical clash between the drys of the temperance movement and the wets, a conflict which continues today.

Although more people in Sweden are drinking than a decade or two ago, they have become more moderate, with the use of more beer and wine and less spirits. The temperance movement continues to be strong and aggressive. It is heavily supported by the government. In recent years about a third of the members of the Swedish parliament are total abstainers, and many others are moderate users. That such persons can be elected to prominent positions says something about the popular attitudes toward alcohol use.

The per capita consumption of alcohol in a given country does not tell us anything of the nature and the amount of alcoholism. The term itself is hard to define, and the definition is bound to vary from one society to another. It seems useful to begin with an interpretation of its meaning in the United States.[9]

The early symptoms of alcoholism in America are often quite unnoticed, even by close friends. Recurrent blackouts, during which the person cannot remember what happened during certain drinking sessions, are some of the first signs. The developing alcoholic has an increasing tolerance for alcohol. He must drink more "to get the same subjective 'glow.' Whereas before, two martinis had produced a feeling of well-being and gregarious friendship, now three or four are required." He begins to sneak drinks furtively, thus deviating from the approved standards of those around him. He begins to have trouble in his work and in family life but tries to cover over such ruptures with renewed efforts to do better. At the same time his drinking is reinforced by alcohol's seeming to help him cope with his social anxieties in adjusting to others.

In what Trice calls the middle phase, the developing alcoholic loses control over his drinking, which is now disrupting his job and his family life. His loss of control is seriously damaging to his self-image. He worries about his employer's suspicions and is concerned about the reactions of his family and his friends. As his loss of control becomes more complete he may resort to lies and excuses, and he may try drinking with a new set of companions.

Yet, since his friends, boss, and family know of his problem, "his guilt and self-hate increase."

A major dimension in the alcoholic's experience is that

> . . . the key people in the alcoholic's life vacillate . . . and hesitate, giving him an opportunity to continue his inexorable march toward the late stage. . . . Slowly they will come to reject him and he them; but, for a crucial time, he receives the sometimes hopeful, sometimes grudging help and tolerance from the "significant others" in his life. When these "others" finally do attempt to apply sanctions, it is usually too late, and the sanctions are too feeble and too irregular. At a time when consistently applied controls (wife could leave, boss could tell him simply and clearly why his work is poor) could define his drinking as a problem and sharply discourage it by decisive action, the wife or boss vacillates, reflecting the traditionally American ambiguous feelings about alcohol. Desperately the alcoholic devises ways to manipulate them into further indecision, and so he progresses further into the middle stages.[10]

He experiences increasing anxiety about his supply of alcohol, on which he has become so dependent. He may hide his supply and sneak more and more drinks. Hangovers now become more awful, with thirst, nausea, headaches, and self-hate magnified. Poor eating leads to loss of weight and may make him vulnerable to diseases related to malnutrition.

His guilt, hopelessness, remorse, and despair now are unbearable—this psychic pain looming much larger than his physical misery.

In the third stage the symptoms are intensified. He is a victim of intense fears that his supply of liquor may be cut off. Hangovers are now very frequent and generally drowned in more alcohol. He is now "completely and absolutely dependent upon alcohol." Delirium tremens, a psychotic condition of terrifying hallucinations, is a serious risk. Socially the alcoholic is now "fully stigmatized, rejected, and labeled."

Trice adds that "most alcoholics spend most of their time in the early and middle stages; but because the late stages are spectacular and often bizarre, alcoholism is popularly thought of in late-stage terms."[11]

Alcoholics in the United States are to be found in all social classes, the lower-class skid-row type being very unrepresentative. Trice quotes research which locates many middle-phase alcoholics in the middle and upper classes. Their drinking is often quite hidden in contrast to that of the lower-classes. They are stable enough to hold their jobs and to maintain their family life although both job and family roles have been severely damaged.

Trice states that the above definition of alcoholism is "relatively peculiar to America. . . . Apparently socio-cultural factors peculiar to America produce vulnerable personalities and segregating forces which isolate heavy-drinking behavior."

The situation is different, for example, in Italy, where nearly everyone drinks alcohol, mostly in the form of wine, with food. There is little or no emotionalism about it; drinking is casually accepted as a part of living. Despite frequent and heavy drinking alcoholism is almost non-existent. In some cases physical symptoms may appear, but because the heavy drinker is brought under group control, not rejected and isolated, psychiatric symptoms of anxiety, isolation, and guilt feelings are absent.

What is the Swedish definition of alcoholism? Swedish legislation of 1913 speaks of "alcohol addiction" and "the danger or grave inconveniences" caused by the behavior of alcohol addicts. In principle, as Daniel Wiklund, a member of the Swedish parliament, has pointed out, "the fundamental basis of this early legislation was protection, and not the care of the alcoholic or a desire to help him."

A new act in 1931 not only stressed protection to community but gave special emphasis to the treatment of alcoholics. The act states that steps shall be taken to guide any person who misuses alcoholic beverages back to a sober way of life. A new legislative act of 1954, supplemented by special statutes in 1955, states:

>The misuser of alcohol must on account of his addiction either
>a. be of danger to another person's security or bodily or mental health or for his own life, or
>b. expose a person, whom it is his duty to support, to suffering or obvious neglect or otherwise fail in his duties towards such a person, or

    c. become a burden to the community, his family or other persons, or

    d. be unable to take care of himself, or

    e. lead a life that is seriously disturbing to neighbors or others.[12]

Some socio-cultural factors with respect to drinking behavior, and the attitudes of others toward it, have been similar in Sweden and in the United States. In both countries there has been a long experience with heavy drinking of strong liquor and a long struggle between wets and drys. In recent decades there has been a strong emphasis in Sweden on helping the heavy drinker to solve some of his interpersonal problems. Much of this is done within his own community so that abusive drinking probably is not generally as socially isolating as it is in the United States. However, as pointed out above, the heavy drinker in Sweden is generally made to feel ashamed and guilty. We would expect the psychiatric symptoms of the alcoholic not to differ greatly from those of the alcoholic in the United States.

A description of the meaning of alcoholism in Sweden, as I learned it from Dr. Nils Jacobson, superintendent of the Clinic for Alcoholic Diseases in Malmö, seems very similar to the process by which alcoholics are produced in the United States:

> It is possible that some of the alcoholics start their careers in a bar. However, since bars are rather exclusive and expensive, most alcoholics do not start this way.
>
> Many alcoholics first start drinking as teenagers at parties and dances. Others begin by drinking with friends at work or during military service. At first drinking may be confined to week ends only, but in time it becomes a daily occurrence.
>
> The drinker may continue at a moderate pace for several years, drinking nearly always with friends. The lone drinker is not common, and he is more likely to manifest psychiatric symptoms from the beginning.
>
> If his drinking becomes more chronic, he will sooner or later have difficulties with his job and with his family. It should also be said that alcoholism may be initiated through trouble with work and family associates. He appears drunk at his job, or he has hangover days when he is absent. He is warned and perhaps dismissed from his job, and his wife may divorce him. He may have considerable difficulties then in locating a new job and a

place to live, particularly if he is lower class. He may end up in a cheap hotel or a compulsory institution for alcoholics. Most alcoholics in Sweden manifest feelings of guilt and anxiety. Swedish alcoholism is based mainly on potato alcohol. Pure beer alcoholism of the Czech type, or wine alcoholism of the French type, is relatively rare.

Keller has estimated that in 1960 there were 3,760,000 men and 710,000 women, a total of 4,470,000, alcoholics in the United States.[13] There is no evidence that the percentage of alcoholics in the United States population has changed significantly since 1960.

TABLE 5

Estimated Alcoholism Rates for Various Countries

| | | | | Estimated Number of Alcoholics | |
| | | | With complications | | With & without complications |
Country	Year	Adults as Percentage of Total Population	Total	per 100,000 adults	per 100,000 adults*
Switzerland	1947	69.8	50,000	1,590	2,385
France	1945	70.6	375,000	1,420	2,850
USA	1948	66.0	952,000	988	3,952
Sweden	1946	71.7	30,800	646	2,580
Denmark	1948	67.4	13,500	487	1,950
Italy	1942	63.3	135,800	476	500
Norway	1947	70.2	8,400	389	1,560
Finland	1947	64.2	8,800	357	1,430
England and Wales	1948	72.0	86,000	278	1,100†

* Varying ratios of "alcoholics with complications" to "all alcoholics" have been assumed on the basis of discussions with experts for the various countries, except for USA, for which the ratio of 1:4 is well established.

† While the estimate of "alcoholics with complications" for England and Wales is probably reliable, the estimate of "all alcoholics" in these countries is hardly better than a guess.

*Source: WHO Technical Report Series, No. 47 (Geneva, Sept., 1961), pp. 19-20.

Estimates of the number of alcoholics and the rate of alcoholics per 100,000 adult population, 20 years and older, for certain countries have been made by the Alcoholism Subcommittee of the World Health Organization.[14] The Jellinek estimation formula[15] was used to estimate the number of alcoholics in the United States by counting the cases who develop the so-called diseases of chronic alcoholism (who in separate United States area studies have approximated 25 per cent of the total alcoholics). It was also applied in the Scandinavian countries because of similar drinking customs. In the other countries listed in Table 5, varying ratios were used in calculating the estimated number of alcoholics in the last column.

According to the estimates in Table 5, Sweden in 1946 had a rate of 2,580 alcoholics, and the United States in 1948 had a rate of 3,952 alcoholics, per 100,000 adults 20 years and over. The rate in the United States was about 50 per cent higher than that in Sweden. There is no evidence indicating that the relative rates between the two countries have changed since the late 1940's. In both countries the per capita consumption of spirits has increased moderately since the 1940's while there has been a large increase in the use of beer and wine.

THE TEMPERANCE MOVEMENT

The organized temperance movement in Sweden has a long history beginning in the 1830's, at about the same time that temperance movements began in the United States. The movement played a large part in initiation of the Bratt system of rationing and in national control of the wholesale and retail traffic in liquor with the possibility of local option. The temperance movement is involved in a widespread educational program in the schools, the military, and the communities. It has sponsored legislation dealing with temperance, such as the act of 1954, which provided for Temperance Boards in every community in Sweden.

Roland Kristiansson, of the Central Union for Temperance Education, introduced me to the temperance program in Sweden. The Central Union is an amalgamation of a number of temperance organizations. The Union disseminates information on problems associated with the use of alcohol and narcotic drugs and, to some extent, on health problems relating to the use of tobacco. The Union produces films, literature, and other materials for use in the schools. It maintains a register of over 700 temperance lecturers available to schools and other interested organizations. These lecturers represent a variety of occupations—businessmen, doctors, social workers, priests, judges, and others. Kristiansson was careful to point out that they must be experts; a vague motivation of wanting to do good will not suffice.

Education in alcohol and drugs is compulsory in the schools. The education is not altogether negative, that is, it does not stress all the bad features of the use of alcohol and counsel students never to drink. Kristiansson stated that the movement considers total abstinence the best approach; if, however, a person does want to drink, he should do so with a sense of responsibility, restraint, and moderation. There is also a temperance educational program in the military. Since all able-bodied young men must spend two years in the military, practically all males in Sweden receive temperance indoctrination.

The temperance organizations in Sweden have nearly half a million members. Although the churches of Sweden, particularly the non-state churches, play a role in the temperance movement, the movement as a whole does not represent a religious and moralistic approach as much as has been true in the United States. As early as 1928 a circular from the King-in-Council stated:

> . . . instruction in temperance shall be to the point, authoritative and objective. It shall be neutral in religious and political points of view. . . . Instruction in temperance should be given in a natural connection with other school subjects. . . . With regard to Training Colleges for Teachers . . . care shall be taken that the special demands of instruction in temperance are properly satisfied, not only in the theoretical, but also in the practical training.

The bulk of the costs of the temperance movement and the facilities for treatment of alcoholics is borne by the central government.

Driving and Alcohol

One of the first things a Swedish host will ask before he serves you a drink is whether you are driving. If you came to his apartment by taxi, or if your wife, who is an abstainer, will drive on the way home, your host will serve you as much liquor as you like. If you yourself will drive, one bottle of weak beer or one small helping of liquor will be the limit. The Swedish law against driving while under the influence of alcohol is strictly enforced, and caution and concern about it seem to be omnipresent among people who drive. Fodor's guide, *Scandinavia,* warns foreign motorists that "no exceptions are made for anyone, so you had better take a taxi if you have been out on the town."

There have been penal provisions against drunkenness at the wheel since 1934. In 1957 legislation provided that "the act of driving a vehicle when affected by alcohol is . . . punishable irrespective of whether or not any injury has been inflicted." It is enough that others be exposed to the possibility of risk to life and limb.

The police periodically stop cars on the highway at random, and drivers must submit to a balloon test. If a test shows some indication of alcohol, the driver must submit to a blood test by a physician. If the blood test shows the presence of alcohol to the extent of 0.8 part per thousand of alcohol in the blood, the penalty will be a fine or imprisonment for not more than six months, even though the alcohol in the blood is not evident in external behavior or lack of control of the vehicle.[16]

A person cannot obtain a driver's license unless he can "provide very clear evidence that he is moderate in his use of alcoholic beverages." The Temperance Board of the applicant's home community must certify that the applicant has a record with respect to the use of alcohol which makes him a suitable person to drive a motor vehicle before the county administration will issue the driver's license. A driver's license may be withdrawn whenever the driver has failed the sobriety test. A person who drives a vehicle daily must in practice abstain almost wholly from alcoholic beverages to be on the right side of the law.

In several American states there is agitation for driver laws similar to those of Sweden. A study reported to the Congress by the United States Department of Transportation in August, 1968, stated some startling research findings:

> The use of alcohol by drivers and pedestrians leads to some 25,000 deaths and a total of at least 800,000 crashes in the United States each year. Especially tragic is the fact that much of the loss in life, limb, and property damage involves completely innocent parties. . . . During the last thirty-five years, in every area of the nation in which the presence and concentrations of alcohol among individuals responsible for initiating crashes have been investigated systematically, alcohol has been found to be the largest single factor leading to fatal crashes. . . . one to four per cent of drivers on the road—those with blood concentrations at or above 100 mg per 100 ml (0.10 by wt)—are accounting for about 50 to 55 per cent of all single vehicle crashes in which drivers are fatally injured. . . . In crashes of all types in which drivers are fatally injured . . . almost half of the drivers . . . have blood alcohol concentration of . . . 0.10 by wt and greater.[17]

Temperance Boards

Community Temperance Boards were first established in Sweden in 1938 but have been greatly increased during subsequent years. The Act of 1954 provided for a Temperance Board for every community. A Board generally consists of seven members selected by the political parties in a given community proportionate to their strength. Both men and women can be members. One member should be a doctor. If there is no local doctor, it is possible that a doctor in the district will sit on several boards. A social welfare assistant frequently does investigative work for the Board into the backgrounds of alcoholics in the community.

In conference with members of several Temperance Boards, I learned that services for persons who have trouble with alcohol are mostly on a voluntary basis. In Sweden as a whole compulsion is used by the Boards in less than 5 per cent of all alcoholic cases; most of the compulsion occurs when individuals are remanded to an institution for treatment. In such cases the Board's action must be approved by the governor of the county.

The Board meets periodically. It considers alcohol problem cases which have come to its attention. Sometimes persons themselves ask for help. In other cases alcohol problems may be reported by a wife or relative or by the police who have made arrests. Board members must accept all reports and evidence as confidential.

At one meeting I raised the question whether alcohol-prone individuals ever resist the Board and become angry about anyone's prying into their affairs. The chairman stated that this sometimes happens but that the Board members are schooled in the ability to "absorb" such aggressions.

Specific Board members are generally assigned to persons having trouble with alcohol, and specific welfare agencies may be activated for certain cases. Often there are family problems and perhaps some disturbances in the neighborhood and at work. The alcohol-prone person may not adjust to his work associates and to work conditions. Some persons are out of work, and the Board does what it can to find suitable employment.

In some serious cases compulsive institutional or out-patient clinical treatment may be required. The Temperance Boards can act when an alcohol addict neglects those whom it is his duty to support, or if he leads a life that is seriously disturbing to his family, neighbors, or work associates, or if he is seriously ill with ailments associated with malnutrition and the toxic accumulations of alcohol. The out-patient approach is becoming more common than institutionalization. Supervision in an institution is generally a matter of confinement for a few months and, except for dangerous persons, at the most for one year.

By far the most important task of the Temperance Boards is to counsel abusers of alcohol, both those in early stages and those who have become addicted. The Boards also give advice on applications for licenses for the sale of alcoholic beverages. They also handle local problems relating to highway traffic and alcohol. It is the duty of the Temperance Boards to inform the county governor about holders of driver's licenses who misuse alcoholic beverages and to certify the sobriety of persons applying for licenses.

INSTITUTIONS FOR ALCOHOLICS

There are 32 public institutions for alcoholics with a total of 2,023 beds. The best-known of these institutions is Venngarn, with 185 places for dangerous and psychopathic alcoholics. The main living and treatment facilities are in a refurbished castle located in a hilly and wooded rural area.

Some 80 per cent of the patients have a background of criminality in which alcohol was involved. The length of stay is determined by the institution and averages four or five months. When they first enter the institution, most of the patients are in poor health. Many have no certain home and have not been working for some time. Most of the patients are from lower classes in the cities. "Country people also drink," the director said, "but on the whole they are less impulsive in their drinking and more moderate, and besides they have relatives and friends who help them out when it comes to illness and unemployment." Intensive medical care is generally necessary during an alcoholic's first weeks in Venngarn. When he is strong and well enough, he will work in a wood- or metal-working shop, hopefully learning the elements of a trade which will be useful when he is released.

All the patients at Venngarn are serious cases and come from all over Sweden. It is the only institution of its kind.

On the day of my visit I asked the director whether the serious cases which came there had a significant rate of cure.

> The rate of cure [he said] is always uncertain. In some cases a man may seem cured, only, sometimes years later, to go back to the abuse of alcohol again. But in any case the institution is doing things for men which should help them work out their personal problems in their communities, which is finally the way it must be done if it is to be done at all. The institution can help restore physical health and train for work which should be a considerable help to the man who is down and out.

Most of the other public institutions for alcoholics, a few of which I visited, are small, open, and secluded in rural areas. They are scattered across Sweden in a way that makes it possible for most patients to be confined near their home communities. All the costs of the 32 public institutions are borne by the national government. Four of these institutions are run directly by the national government, whereas others are managed by welfare agencies, counties, and cities. In addition, there are 14 private institutions with about 300 beds. The private institutions are similar to convalescent homes at which only voluntary patients are received. The state defrays most of the cost.

In addition, there are facilities for housing and treating alcoholics within some communities where patients receive treatment while they continue to work at their usual places of employment. Sometimes these facilities are used for aftercare for certain institutional cases.

Drunks and Their Treatment

The police may jail, for not more than four hours, a person accused of being drunk in public. Typically such a drunk is fined the equivalent of about ten dollars when brought before a magistrate.

Dr. Bengt Bergren, psychiatrist in charge of the center for the treatment of alcoholics at Uppsala, has been developing a project for the treatment of drunks in which he has sought to minimize the criminalistic type of handling given by the police when they arrest a drunk and lock him up. During a visit with Bergren he said:

> The police generally use some strong-arm tactics, push a man into a cell where he may then have physical-psychological reactions, such as vomiting and becoming hostile.
> The police have the man come up for a fine and then report the case to his local Temperance Board, which is obliged to contact the person.
> My experiment has run over a period of several months during which a total of 333 patients have been brought to the hospital unit which I operate. If the patient is of the "tough variety," someone who cannot be handled here, he is sent back. Actually, of the 333 only five had to be sent back.
> I have a staff of nurses and social workers with whom I have worked rather intensively to develop a humane understanding attitude toward drunks. The drunk must not be tied up or put in an isolation cell. No matter what happens, the treatment must

involve human relations and medical attention. Contacts with people and nursing care are important. The personnel must be willing to absorb a man's anxieties and hostilities. Ordinarily the staff, as well as the police, may be inclined to want to tell a patient to go to hell with his kind of behavior.

It has been very difficult to train a staff that can work patiently with the drunks, but we think it is working out. Of the 333 intakes, we have been able to dismiss 270 in a day or so, some even within a few hours. Only four of the 333 thus far received have vomited. None of them has struck any blows, and there has been no physical damage.

Although Swedish police are quite well trained, they are nevertheless inclined to handle a drunk in a relatively rough way. Police typically think that to use psychiatry or psychology in treatment is theoretical and irresponsible. We have worked with the police, and we think we have won some of them over to our type of approach. The police are now much more cooperative than they were at first. They have become interested in what the staff is trying to do. About a fourth of the drunks we have handled are first offenders so far as arrest is concerned. The rest have been arrested for drunkenness a number of times, some as many as ten times or more.

We think that when a man leaves here, the hope for productive counseling by his Temperance Board and by others will be better.

Bergren was critical of some of the Temperance Boards. He said they did not place enough stress on the early symptoms of an individual in trouble with alcohol. They made it a point to talk with him when they saw some troubles arising but did not often enough take action that involved real treatment. There was a tendency to not want to "get things stirred up too much." Bergren thought there were too many cases which kept developing until they became chronic, when often the development could have been "nipped in the bud" in the early stages.

INTERPRETATION

Connery, who has studied the Swedish way of life for many years, thinks the Swedes are learning to space their drinking in Continental fashion rather than saving it for all-out Nordic binges. He thinks Sweden's 200-year hangover is finished.[18]

Although a sizable amount of aquavit, the traditional favorite, is still being produced in Sweden, there has nevertheless been a swing away from it to beer and wine. Table 6 indicates the long-term trend.

The change in the types of alcoholic beverages, and in the manner of their use, is a change similar to what has been occurring in the United States. It has not prevented or removed all the problems of alcoholism—problems which will probably endure to the end of time; however, the change in types of beverages, together with the spacing of drinks, can be interpreted as a swing toward moderation for the great majority of drinkers.

TABLE 6

Annual Consumption in Gallons Per Inhabitant of Alcoholic Beverages

Year	Spirits	Wines	Beer
1861-65	2.8	.10	2.9
1866-70	2.2	.1	2.8
1871-75	3.1	.2	3.9
1876-80	2.6	.18	4.5
1881-85	2.1	.18	4.9
1886-90	1.8	.13	6.1
1891-95	1.7	.15	6.8
1896-00	2.1	.18	8.2
1901-05	2.0	.15	7.9
1906-10	1.7	.13	6.9
1911-15	1.7	.13	. 5.6
1916-20	.87	.23	4.43
1921-25	1.1	.13	5.9
1926-30	1.2	.23	6.6
1931-35	1.1	.2	6.0
1936-40	1.1	.23	6.4
1941-45	1.0	.2	5.2
1946-50	1.32	.36	6.2
1951-55	1.37	.44	7.1
1956-60	1.37	.73	7.3
1961-65	1.32	1.0	8.1
1966	1.4	1.2	9.9
1967	1.42	1.3	10.7
1968	1.34	1.4	12.3

Source: National Board of Excise, Stockholm.

The number of drinkers, particularly among women and young people, has increased in Sweden in recent decades. However, the average amount per capita consumption of pure alcohol has not changed appreciably. We assume this to mean that heavy drinking by those using mainly spirits has diminished. This is in line with interpretation of similar changes in the types of alcoholic beverages consumed in the United States. Jellinek has stated that

> A large consumption of distilled spirits and a small consumption of beer is generally an indication that the users are relatively few in number but individually heavy consumers. A large consumption of beer, on the other hand, is indicative of a wide use and relatively small individual consumption.[19]

The change in drinking patterns has been deliberately promoted by the temperance movement and governmental controls on the traffic in alcoholic beverages. It is nevertheless difficult to know just what has brought the "200-year-old binge" to an end. The many governmental controls and restrictions on the production and sale of alcohol no doubt have some relationship to the changed pattern of drinking, although it is impossible to know to what extent these controls have caused the big change. Sweden has long borders, so that alcohol no doubt could be smuggled in and illegal private production could take place if the craving for alcohol were strong enough and governmental restrictions on consumption too severe.

The fact that it is illegal to advertise alcoholic beverages and that private profit motivations are nil probably plays only a minor role in producing the changes in consumption of alcohol. The significance of this factor is, however, impossible to measure.

The temperance movement, particularly the program of community Temperance Boards, must have some relationship to the change in alcohol consumption. The existence of the Temperance Boards is based largely on the assumption that deviant drinking develops as a result of difficulties in interpersonal relations in the community. It is consistent with a theory of alcoholism which has been emerging in the United States, namely, that alcoholism is basically not a "disease" but the result of insufficient "consensus regarding behavioral definitions of alcohol to achieve a degree of control of individual use that satisfies the group." [20]

Dr. Harold Mulford, director of Alcoholic Studies, University of Iowa, points out that the popular disease concept of alcoholism often takes the alcoholic out of the community and puts him in the hands of a doctor, clinic, or hospital. Actually it is ultimately in the interpersonal relations in the community that the problems of the alcoholic must be solved. Medicinal attention, to be sure, has a responsibility to manage or treat the varied physical results of alcoholism, such as malnutrition and cirrhosis of the liver. Deviant drinking relates to cultural norms and human relations, and the doctor can do little or nothing to manage or change such norms and relations. "Only through interaction with others," says Mulford, "is the problem drinker likely to redefine his situation and develop a way of looking at things—usually called 'motivation'—and to obtain the necessary social support for such 'motivation' to correct his drinking and related behavior."[21]

To the extent that the Temperance Boards take a dogmatic approach and emotionalize the drinking issue, they may actually produce more problem drinkers rather than fewer. In my visits with Temperance Boards and individual Board members, I was impressed with the emphasis they placed on aiding the problem drinker with his personal relations to others. They counsel with him and seek to motivate him to help himself in his readjustment to members of the family, neighbors, and work associates. To the extent that the Boards are successful in this endeavor, deviant drinking and alcohol consumption should be reduced.

The Temperance Boards seem to be based on rather sound sociological principles and have no doubt had a degree of success in the reduction of problem drinking.

The change toward more temperate use of alcohol in Sweden has been most evident in the last one hundred years, coinciding with the time that urbanism and industrial technology have been developing rapidly. Research by Seeley[22] shows that the more urban states and provinces in the United States and Canada have higher rates of alcoholism than the more rural. Trice points out, however, that the rural-urban differences reported in such studies

. . . may be due to under-reporting in rural areas and more accurate reports in large towns and cities. In rural sections, concern about the social stigma of a patient may prevent physicians from labeling a person an alcoholic. Also, one of the indexes used to estimate the prevalence of alcoholism—cirrhosis of the liver—may often be missed unless an autopsy is performed—an action taken less in small towns than in urban areas.[23]

We have noted, however, that long before urbanism there was much heavy drinking in Sweden, a phenomenon in which the humble potato as an easy source of alcohol played an important role. In earlier centuries rural life and work did not have as many technological and community factors which could delimit heavy drinking and periodic drunkenness. This was particularly true for men. When a farmer went on an alcoholic binge, his work on the farm, particularly in the winter, could often be carried on by his wife and children so that income was not greatly impaired.

The situation is entirely different in an urban-industrial age. We have previously noted the role of labor-union leaders in the promotion of temperance among union members; they discovered quite early that unions could not be effective if many of the members were periodically drunk. We have also noted that Sweden, with heavy traffic on the highways and streets, has taken strong measures to keep drinkers from driving. Moreover, the holders of modern business, governmental, and professional positions cannot perform their roles effectively if heavy drinking is involved. Such roles demand the coordination of the activities of many people and generally require alert attention and many decisions.

The worker in modern factories and shops can also be immobilized by deviant drinking. If he works with dangerous machines, or with machines requiring close attention and coordination, drinking on the job can quickly handicap him. If he misses work because of alcoholic binges, there is generally no one in the family who can carry on for him, as is possible on the farm, so that his regular income is impaired, if not ended. Shop clerks and professional persons, whose work constantly involves dealing with the general public, can also impair their positions and incomes rather quickly with the impulsive use of alcohol.

A technological society cannot reach a high degree of achievement, such as Sweden has done, with large amounts of uncontrolled drinking. Similar things can be said for the United States, where high technological achievement would be impossible if the drinking mores were still the same as those of frontier days.

Although the total rates of alcoholism have declined in the last hundred years in both Sweden and the United States, both countries still have significant numbers of problem drinkers, and the reasons are somewhat similar. In each country there has been a long dry-wet struggle which has charged the alcohol issue with high emotional overtones. In neither country has there developed as yet a sufficient general understanding and agreement regarding what beverages may be drunk, and when, by whom, and on what occasions. This is particularly true in the United States, a larger country, which has inherited the norms of many ethnic groups which are reflected in the variability of laws and ordinances in the different states and cities.

In countries with low rates of alcoholism, such as Italy, people generally consume most of their alcoholic beverages with meals. A survey has shown that only 1 per cent of Italians drink other than at mealtimes.[24] Alcohol is taken in a matter-of-fact way as part of life, with no pressure on people either to drink or not to drink. There are strong taboos on drunkenness, however.

Among Jews in the United States "the rules of drinking are well defined." Wine is used as part of religious and family observances and ". . . the whole family, including young children, participates in this ceremonial use of alcohol."[25] Drunkenness is strongly disapproved. Attitudes developed in the ceremonial use of alcohol tend to carry over into social drinking.

Among most other Americans there is less clarity about the appropriate and inappropriate patterns of drinking. Usually drinking is defined as "having fun" or is escapist and is not necessarily associated with other activities, such as religious ceremonies or eating. There are many uncertainties in the United States about whether children and youth should be allowed to drink at all. Often, as Plant points out, "for some youngsters the first drinking experience is an act of rebellion." Research has demonstrated that rebellious drinking often leads to serious problem drinking.[26]

Both the cultures which are highly permissive and those which are highly restrictive about the use of alcohol seem to be ineffective in the prevention of alcoholism. However, in both Sweden and the United States the emphasis is increasingly on moderation and self-control rather than on complete abstinence or complete freedom of use. The emotional charge relating to the alcohol issue has been reduced. Drinking has become more moderate and controlled than in earlier rural cultures. The demands of a highly complex urban-industrial society with high standards of living are incompatible with uncontrolled drinking and widespread alcoholism.

NOTES

1. Gunnar Dahlberg, "A Note on Drinking and Drunkards in Sweden," *Acta Genetica Et Statistica Medica,* Vol. 2 (1951), p. 36.
2. Nils Christie, "Scandinavian Hangover," *Trans-Action,* Vol. 4, No. 3, pp. 35 f.
3. Donald Connery, *The Scandinavians* (New York: Simon & Schuster, 1966), p. 424.
4. Kettil Bruun & Ragnar Hauge, *Drinking Habits Among Northern Youth* (Helsinki, Finland: Suomalaisen Kirjallisund en Kirjapaino Oy).
5. *Ibid.,* p. 89.
6. *Ibid.,* pp. 58 f.
7. Nils Sunberg, "The Alcohol Question in Sweden" (unpublished ms.), p. 4.
8. *Ibid.*
9. Harrison M. Trice, *Alcoholism in America* (New York: McGraw-Hill), pp. 28 ff. Used by permission.
10. *Ibid.,* pp. 34 f.
11. *Ibid.,* p. 36.
12. Daniel Wiklund, *The Swedish System for Prevention of Alcoholism and Treatment of Alcoholics* (Lausanne, Switzerland: International Commission for the Treatment of Alcoholics), p. 14.
13. Mark Keller, "The Definition of Alcoholism and the Estimation of Its Prevalence," in David J. Pittman & Charles R. Snyder, eds., *Society, Culture, and Drinking Patterns* (New York: Wiley, 1962).
14. WHO Technical Report Series, No. 47 (Geneva, Switzerland), Sept., 1961, pp. 19-20.
15. E. M. Jellinek, "Recent Trends in Alcoholism and Alcohol Consumption," *Quarterly Journal of Studies on Alcohol,* Vol. 8 (1947).

16. Sundberg, pp. 17 f.

17. *Alcohol and Highway Safety Report* (Washington: Govt. Printing Office, 1968), pp. 1, 11-14.

18. Connery, p. 9.

19. Jellinek, p. 9.

20. See excellent statement of this theory by Harold A. Mulford, "Alcoholism, A Concern (and Creation) of Every Community," *Selected Papers,* 18th Annual Meeting, NAAAP (Chicago, 1967), pp. 3-15.

21. Mulford, p. 10.

22. John R. Seeley, "WHO Definition of Alcoholism," *Quarterly Journal of Studies on Alcohol,* Vol. 20, pp. 353-58.

23. Trice, pp. 40 f. Used by permission.

24. Thomas F. A. Plant, for the Cooperative Commission on the Study of Alcoholism, *Alcohol Problems* (Oxford Univ. Press, 1967), pp. 127 f.

25. *Ibid.,* p. 26.

26. *Ibid.,* pp. 129 ff.

V

Drug Abuse

In recent years there has been a large increase of drug abuse in Sweden. An extended visit with Professor Gunnar Inghe of the Medical College of the Karolina Institute of Stockholm introduced me to the problem. Inghe is a member of the World Health Organization and of the Narcotics Drug Committee of the Swedish National Medical Board. He said:

> Sweden has never really had a problem of drug addiction of the classical type, that is, in which derivatives of opium such as heroin and morphine are used. Several decades ago there were only a few persons using such drugs, and the users were mostly members of the medical profession and patients who had received the drugs to relieve chronic pain. Even today there are relatively few users of the opiates, but some users are now to be found in youth and criminal groups.
>
> The bigger problem is with the drugs which are stimulants to the central nervous system, mainly the amphetamines and the phenmetrazines. Technically these are not narcotic drugs, that is, they do not induce a dulling of the senses. However, from a legal point of view, narcotic drugs are defined as those drugs whose manufacture and sales are regulated by international or national conventions and which have certain characteristics such as a compulsion to continue, a psychic and/or physical dependence, and "withdrawal distress" when use is discontinued.
>
> The use of the stimulant drugs began slowly. There were some cases just before World War II. During, and immediately after the war such drugs were used mostly by artists and musicians and by so-called Bohemian groups.
>
> But other people—students, housewives, truck drivers, and others—also began to try them. In 1939 they were placed on the prescription list as one means of control.
>
> The highest sales were in the larger cities and in the university towns. In the early 1940's it was estimated that there were about 200,000 users of amphetamines. Only about 200 were

estimated to be "excessive users." Most of the users took the drug one to four times a year.

By the early 1950's the use of stimulant drugs had increased and began to appear in juvenile gangs. Within the last five years the rate of growth has been considerable, and it continues to increase. In 1959 some of the stimulant drugs were designated as "narcotics" by national law and pronounced illegal except in medical prescriptions. This led to an illegal trade in the drugs, with falsified prescriptions, peddling, and theft from pharmacies.

The amphetamines and phenmetrazines are bought in tablet form, dissolved in water, and injected intravenously into the blood. An addict typically takes from 50 to 200 tablets a day.

The stimulant drugs create feelings of expansiveness, great excitement and an enormous feeling of happiness. The individual becomes garrulous and highly active, getting no real rest or sleep sometimes for several days at a time. There is no evidence that the drugs stimulate sex or violence. They inhibit the appetite and even the desire for water. In a day or two the user is generally unable to talk, his mouth is very dry, and he feels exhausted and sleepy. Some users experience fear, anxiety, restlessness and nightmares. A strong psychic dependence on stimulant drugs may develop, particularly for the users of phenmetrazines. A paranoid reaction sometimes appears in which the individual has the illusion of being pursued or tormented by police or other persons, sometimes by his friends.

Not all who try the stimulant drugs go back to them. But there are those who do. They may find the world rather prosaic, hard and dull without drugs. Gradually the drugs become a kind of mental crutch without which it is hard to face realities. The drugs do not develop body tolerance as in the case of the opiates, but there may be the development of a strong psychological and social dependence. This is particularly likely if the user is in a subculture which defines the drug as a "good thing," as a way of "opening the mind," of "understanding things which otherwise cannot be understood," and as a way whereby one may be "set off from ordinary mortals."

The subculture also develops techniques of how to use the drugs, and where and how to obtain them. Moreover, it may give a sense of identity to an individual who feels more or less rejected by society.

The use of stimulant drugs is found mainly among persons in their twenties. About one-fourth of the criminals arrested by the police in recent years are users. There are users who must steal to keep themselves supplied with drugs. Some have said that stimulant drugs make them more bold and daring for the commission of thefts and other crimes. In the last few years the use of the drugs has been increasing among teenagers and its incidence is increasing among women in crime.

SURVEYS OF INCIDENCE OF DRUG ABUSE

The Swedish Narcotic Drugs Committee has made an extensive analysis of a variety of studies of the narcotics problem in Sweden. Their findings have been written up by Professor Leonard Goldberg, M.D., and published in the *Bulletin on Narcotics*. This present brief résumé on incidence studies is based on these published materials.[1]

Hospital Cases

A nationwide point prevalence study was undertaken by the Narcotic Drugs Committee of all hospital patients treated on a certain date in 1966. Five hundred and fifty-six drug-dependent persons—339 men and 217 women—were reported as in-patients on the day studied. The males averaged 36.7 years; the females averaged 37.3. The marital status of the drug users differed considerably from that of the general population, with a far greater proportion of the users being single, divorced, or widowed. Sixty-nine per cent used hypnotics and tranquilizers. Opiates were used by a minority of 4 per cent, while 18 per cent used stimulants. The choice of drugs was affected considerably by the age of the users. Among the youngest, 10-19 years, abuse of industrial solvents, such as glue and paint thinner, dominated, while stimulant drugs were next. In the 20-29 age group, hypnotics and stimulant drugs dominated, whereas in the 30-39 age group, the drugs most frequently abused were sedatives and tranquilizers. Hypnotics dominated among those over 40. Members of lower classes predominated among the hospital cases of abusers.

Schoolchildren

In 1967 the National Board of Schools made a nationwide survey of drug use among schoolchildren with an 11 per cent sample for ages 14 to 19. Inhalation of volatile solvents by sniffing was concentrated in the lower ages. Nineteen per cent of all pupils said they knew of others in their schools who were taking drugs. Fifteen and nine-tenths per cent said they had been offered drugs. Of those offered drugs, "64 per cent were offered cannabis, 20 per cent stimulants, 7 per cent LSD, and 9 per cent unknown drugs." Ninety-five and one-tenth per cent had never taken drugs.

One and five-tenths per cent were presently taking drugs, a total of 2,040 pupils. Of these, 75 per cent were smoking cannabis, 7 per cent were using LSD, 9 per cent stimulant drugs, and 9 per cent hypnotics or tranquilizers. Of the total sample of school-children for Sweden, 3.5 per cent had used or were presently using drugs.

The pattern of drug abuse among Stockholm schoolchildren was essentially the same as for children from all of Sweden except that the proportion of users was much higher in the Stockholm survey, 18.9 per cent as against 3.5 per cent for all of Sweden.

Goldberg estimates that there are about 100 to 150 groups of five to ten members each among the lower-class boys in Stockholm, or a total of 400 to 600 persons. They tend to form subcultures and concentrate in certain areas where their drug use is associated with prostitution and theft. Another type of subculture prevails among groups of "intellectuals, or quasi-intellectuals, artists [and] students." Aside from the illegal use of drugs these groups are not characterized by criminal culture or antisocial behavior.

Goldberg states that the total of drug abusers in Sweden may be between 5,000 and 7,000.

WHY THE EMERGENCE OF DRUG ABUSE?

There are no certain answers to the question why drug abuse has increased in Sweden or in any other country.

We can say that there have been many developments in chemistry which have isolated numerous new "mind-changing" drugs. This is a necessary condition for the drugs to be used, but it does not tell us why people use the drugs when they appear. Life in the industrial-urban age may have some facets which tend to make people more willing to try new things, including drugs, or it may impose certain social-psychological distress and anxiety, making mind-changing drugs welcome when they appear.

However, we have no way of knowing how people might have reacted to these drugs if they had appeared a hundred years ago. Life in rural Sweden, before the modern era, imposed many hardships, with recurrent food shortages and frequent wars. There were few conveniences, and there was much hard labor. If the early reception of alcohol in rural Sweden is any clue, we can surmise that drugs would have had as much play then as now if they had been available.

Once a certain amount of drug abuse has been started, the habit tends to feed on itself. In the case of the opiates body tolerance develops after a few months of use, requiring larger and larger doses to prevent withdrawal distress. It may be that body tolerance, or in any case a strong psychological dependence, is also characteristic of the stimulant drugs, judging by the way users increase their doses. A therapeutic dose of stimulant drugs is said to be no more than two or three tablets daily; the stimulant-drug user typically increases his intake until he consumes 50 to 200 tablets daily.

The traffic in drugs can be very profitable, especially when it is dominated by powerful crime syndicates as in the United States. As in most business the individuals and organizations that deal with drugs may try to increase their market by developing more customers. Retailers, who are sometimes users of drugs themselves, invite newcomers to give it a try until some of them become steady customers.

Assessor C. E. Sturkell, of Sweden's Ministry of Social Affairs, has suggested several additional reasons why the misuse of drugs started late relative to other Western nations but increased rapidly once it started.[2] He points out that Sweden experienced urbanization and industrialization at a later date in history than other Western countries, and that experience has shown that narcotics abuse grows and spreads most rapidly in densely populated areas. Also, the relative affluence of Sweden has attracted a large number of immigrant workers to Sweden in recent years, particularly from Southern Europe, some of the newcomers bringing narcotic drugs with them. Furthermore, the large incomes of Swedish families have made a potential market for the purchase of drugs. Swedes travel rather extensively to Spain and Italy, two countries which manufacture stimulant drugs in large quantities and which have not yet imposed any restrictions on their use or export.

There is no evidence that a powerful organization handles the drug traffic in Sweden. The traffic is handled by small amateur groups through theft from pharmacies, doctors' offices, and hospitals and through smuggling from other countries while traveling as tourists.

COMPARATIVE DRUG ABUSE IN THE UNITED STATES

It is almost impossible to make meaningful comparisons of the incidence and culture of drug abuse between the United States and Sweden.

Earlier Use

Opium has been known in the United States from colonial times. Morphine was isolated in 1812, and heroin was first produced in 1898. The opiates were used by the medical profession in the treatment of symptoms of a wide variety of disorders. Their use was widespread, particularly in the last half of the 19th century, when they were prescribed for such disorders as diarrhea and gynecologic conditions. Patent medicines often contained opium, morphine, or codeine. Many patients became addicted.[3]

The use of drugs in 19th-century United States was more by whites than by Negroes and somewhat more by middle- and upper-status persons than by lower classes. Two-thirds of the users may have been women. Addicts were mostly of middle age. Addiction by juveniles was rare. There were no strong public attitudes against the use of drugs. During most of the 19th century, drugs and addiction were less associated with the underworld and smuggling organizations than at present.[4]

When criminals became involved in the drug traffic, public opinion began to change. Stern laws and regulations began to appear in the early 20th century.

Present-day Use

The present pattern of drug abuse in the United States is very different from that of the 19th century. The average addict is younger than users in the 19th century. An increasing number of juveniles are involved.

In 1966 the Federal Bureau of Narcotics reported 60,000 active drug addicts in the United States. Not all addicts are known or reported, so that only estimates can be made of their number. O'Donnell and Ball suggest 60,000 to 100,000 addicts as a reasonable estimate. These are basically addicted to heroin. The estimates do not include a count of all abusers of such drugs as marijuana, amphetamines, LSD, and industrial solvents, such as glue and paint thinner.

The known addicts are mostly in the largest cities. Over half of those reported by the Narcotics Bureau are from New York City. Large numbers are in Los Angeles, Chicago, Detroit, Washington, Philadelphia, Newark, San Diego, San Antonio, and San Francisco. Male addicts outnumber female addicts about 4 or 5 to 1. Most addicts are young adults. Many users have minority-group status, particularly Negro, Puerto Rican, and Mexican-American. Most addicts are unemployed or in illegal activities or in lower-status jobs.[5]

Some of the newspaper and magazine accounts of sprees of drug abuse occurring in schools and colleges of the United States sound very similar to Swedish reports of drug abuse among children and youth. A recent newspaper story about drug abuse in a midwestern city stated that youth reported such incidents as the following:

> . . . a recent suicide by a young man in his early 20's took place during an LSD party. [Several other recent deaths of young people who were drug users are believed to have been associated with drug use.]
> A 17-year-old [recently] . . . admitted breaking into a drug-

store and stealing $142.00 in prescription drugs. A number of young people have been in and out of psychiatric wards . . . as a direct result of their use of drugs. Dr.—— [a psychiatrist, reported that] . . . "two years ago it was rare to see a local youth hospitalized in connection with the use of drugs. It has greatly increased over the last two years."

. . . —— High School, which enjoys a well-deserved reputation of both academic and athletic excellence, was on the defensive. . . . A survey showed that nearly half of its students drink outside their homes. More than one out of ten admitted they have smoked marihuana, and six students said they had done so within the school building. More than one out of 20 said they had engaged in glue sniffing. . . . One out of 20 said they had used other drugs.

Dr. —— [a local psychiatrist] said he has observed marked increases in the past year in hospital admissions for psychiatric treatment of young patients using drugs. Some of these, he said, are 12 and 13 years of age, but most are 16, 17, and 18 years old . . . most have been in from the effects of glue sniffing, but others have been in for amphetamines and barbiturates. He states that he hears quite a bit of talk about heroin, but has not confronted it in [this city].

In the same city a lay theologian estimates that more than half the teen-agers were engaged in either drinking, illicit sex, glue sniffing, or marijuana smoking.

An instructor at the local community college states that he "sometimes finds half the class 'glassy eyed' from drugs."

[It may be added that the city in question] . . . has the highest per capita and per family income in the state. . . . The schools enjoy national renown for academic excellence and high school students regularly score above the state and national average on college entrance exams.

[Some users] stated that the nearby University Campus is a good source for marijuana, LSD and other drugs.[6]

NOTES

1. United Nations, Vol. XX, No. 1 (Jan.-March, 1968), pp. 1-36, and No. 2 (April-June, 1968), pp. 9-35.

2. As reported by Ronald Aqua in an unpublished manuscript, "Sweden and the Narcotics Question."

3. John A. O'Donnell & John C. Ball, eds., *Narcotic Addiction* (New York: Harper & Row, 1966), p. 1.

4. Alfred R. Lindesmith & John H. Gagnon, "Anomie and Drug Addiction," in Marshall B. Clinard, ed., *Anomie and Deviant Behavior: A Discussion and a Critique* (New York: Free Press, 1964), pp. 164 f.

5. O'Donnell & Ball, p. 10.

6. Des Moines *Register,* Nov. 24, 1968.

VI

Suicide

Americans seem to raise more questions about suicide in Sweden than about any other form of deviant behavior except sex freedom. Some hint darkly at socialism and welfarism; others think the long, cold winters may be to blame. Still others guess

TABLE 7

Death Rates for Various Countries From Suicide in 1961-63 (yearly average) for Each Sex and Both Sexes, From 15 Years of Age, per 100,000 Population

Country	Both Sexes	Yearly Average Rates Male	Female	Excess Male*
Austria	28.3	42.0	16.9	249
Canada	11.1	17.3	4.9	353
Czechoslovakia	28.2	40.9	16.5	248
Denmark	24.2	32.4	16.2	200
England and Wales	15.1	18.3	12.2	150
Finland	29.0	47.7	12.3	388
France	20.7	32.3	10.0	323
Germany (Federal Republic)	24.1	33.3	16.2	206
Hungary	33.9	48.9	20.3	241
Israel (Jewish population)	10.1	11.9	8.2	145
Italy	7.1	10.2	4.2	243
Japan	24.7	29.0	20.6	141
Netherlands	9.1	11.5	6.8	169
Norway	10.0	15.7	4.5	349
Poland	12.8	21.9	4.7	466
Sweden	21.7	32.0	11.6	276
Switzerland	23.3	33.9	13.2	257
U.S.A.	15.6	24.0	7.7	312

*Number of male suicides for every 100 female suicides.

Source: World Health Organization **Prevention of Suicide** (Geneva, 1968), p. 69.

Suicide   113

that the Swedes are perhaps characterized by a morbid introverted temperament of a kind which is fertile ground for suicide.

The critics are surprised to learn that Sweden does not have the highest suicide rate in the world or even in Europe. Table 7 indicates that Austria, Czechoslovakia, Denmark, Finland, West Germany, Hungary, and Switzerland have higher rates than Sweden. Outside of Europe, Japan has higher rates.

Table 7 indicates the number of male suicides for every 100 female suicides for each country. The average number of male suicides per 100 female suicides is 250. The Swedish ratio is 276.

Table 8 shows the long-term trends of suicide rates in Sweden

TABLE 8

Suicide Rates in Sweden, 1900-67, and in U.S., 1900-66, Per 100,000 Population

Year	Sweden Rate	U.S. Rate	Year	Sweden Rate	U.S. Rate
1905	14.6	13.5	1954	16.9	10.1
1915	14.2	16.2	1955	17.7	10.2
1925	12.9	12.0	1956	20.1	10.0
1935	16.0	14.3	1957	19.9	9.8
1945	13.6	11.2	1958	17.2	10.7
1946	14.8	11.5	1959	18.1	10.4
1947	14.3	11.5	1960	17.4	10.6
1948	14.2	11.2	1961	16.9	10.4
1949	16.0	11.4	1962	18.4	10.9
1950	14.9	11.4	1963	18.4	11.0
1951	16.1	10.4	1964	19.7	10.8
1952	16.7	10.0	1965	19.2	11.1
1953	18.5	10.1	1966	20.0	10.8
			1967	21.6	

Sources: Sweden: 1905-50 **Historical Statistics of Sweden,** Table 141. 1951-55 **Historical Statistics of Sweden,** Table 311. 1956-67 **Statistical Abstract of Sweden, 1968,** Table 310.

United States: 1905-34 Office of Vital Statistics. 1935-65 **Facts of Life and Death,** U.S. Dept. of Health, Education, and Welfare, 1967, Table 20. 1966 rate computed from total number of suicides and total population in **Statistical Yearbook, 1967.**

and in the United States. The rates in Sweden during the 19th century were relatively low, although during that century the rate rose 515 per cent. According to a study quoted by Durkeim, France, Prussia, Denmark, Saxony, and Austria had higher rates than Sweden during the period 1866-78 covered by the study.[1] The Swedish rate has increased approximately 75 per cent since 1900 to its present level. The United States rate rose from 10.2 in 1900 to a high of 16.2 in 1915 and thereafter declined to 10.8 in 1966. Figure 1 compares the Swedish and American suicide rates in graphic form.

THE PROBLEM OF SUICIDE REPORTING

The exact number of suicides in a given country cannot be known. There are reasons to believe that they are generally underestimated. One difficulty is that it is sometimes hard to distinguish between an accident and a suicide. The suicide data in the United States are based mostly on coroners' reports. Since coroners are generally not trained in medical diagnosis, many of their verdicts are inconclusive. Dublin estimates that the number of suicides in the United States is probably higher by as much as one-fourth or one-third than that actually recorded.[2]

In Western countries suicide is generally considered to be a disgrace. It was defined as reprehensible early in Christian history. It is believed that the Christian has an obligation to live his life; to do away with it has been considered the same as murder. Throughout medieval times suicides were punished with excommunication and dishonorable interment; suicide was believed to be a sin which could never be forgiven. These practices and beliefs still persist in some Catholic countries.[3] Although the older views have moderated somewhat in Protestant countries and areas, suicide is still considered shameful.

Such attitudes about suicide can operate to make the accuracy of the official rates of suicide questionable. A family may try to hide a suicide by making it look like an accident. Priests or local authorities are sometimes willing to cover up for the family.

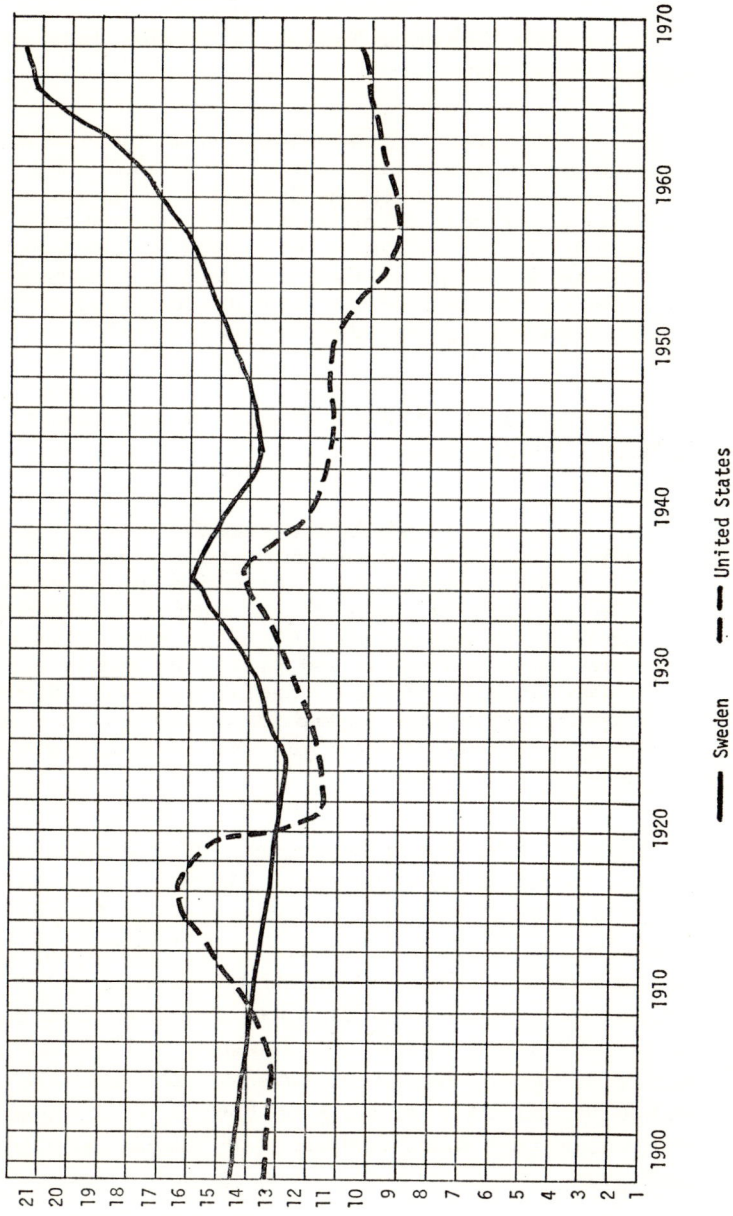

Figure 1

Comparison of United States and Swedish Suicide Rates per 100,000 population

Sources: Tables 7 and 8

Sweden   United States

In his study "Suicide in Sweden, 1925-1950," Hans Hartelius states his belief that

> . . . the Swedish official statistics on the causes of death are probably among the most reliable in the world. Civil registration is known to be reliable, death certifications are obligatory in towns and are becoming increasingly common in rural districts as well, and, at any rate in the country, the clergy have good personal knowledge of their parishioners. Consequently data regarding individual suicides reach the central registers for the whole country together with the cause of death.[4]

In a letter to me, Dr. K. G. Dahlgren of the Psychiatric Clinic in Malmö, Sweden, states:

> . . . in countries which have a negative view on suicides and where medico-legal autopsies are not . . . regularly made we have reason to suspect that many suicides are registered under other diagnoses for causes of death such as "intoxication" and "accident." As medico-legal autopsies are more seldom made in Norway than in Denmark and Sweden, this may be one of the reasons for the low figure for suicides in Norway. Figures from countries in which the Anglo-Saxon coroner system is used can hardly be directly compared with countries using a medico-legal system.

Hartelius states that in Sweden, as in other Western countries, suicide "is considered reprehensible, immoral, shameful, or at least lamentable." However, owing to the high level of public education and to religion's seeming quite irrelevant in Sweden, one may doubt whether the stigma on suicide is as strong in Sweden as in some countries where strong religious opinions prevail. We would expect more frankness and openness about suicides in Sweden. The records have been kept since 1785; there is, however, no way of knowing just how the Swedish and American suicide rates would compare if all suicides were tabulated each year.

TABLE 9

Suicides in Sweden by Age & Sex 1956-67

Age	No. Both Sexes		Per Cent of Total
24 & under	1,160		6.74
25-44	4,980		28.97
45 & over	11,050		64.28

Total No. of Suicides	Male	Female	Female Per Cent of Total
17,190	12,828	4,362	25.37

Source: Computed from **Statistical Abstract of Sweden, 1968,** Table 310.

Table 9 makes it evident that age is an important element in suicide in Sweden as it is in all Western countries. Less than 7 per cent of all suicides in 1956 through 1967 were 24 years old and under. About 29 per cent were 25 to 44, and almost two-thirds were 45 and over. During the same period male suicides outnumbered female suicides about 3 to 1.

In the United States the suicide rate for persons 45 years and over in 1964 was 20 per 100,000 as compared with 10.8 for all ages. The rate for males in 1964 was 16.1 as compared with 5.6 for females.

Tables 10 and 11 show that suicide also relates to the marital state in both Sweden and the United States. Since the time suicide records have been kept in Western countries, the married have had lower rates than the unmarried, the widowed, and the divorced. In Tables 10 and 11 the divorced have higher rates than persons in any other marital-status category.

Marital State

TABLE 10

Suicides in Sweden by Sex, Marital Status, Rural/Urban, 1951-63

Rural Men		Rate per 100,000
	Unmarried	38.63
	Married	27.09
	Widowed	66.73
	Divorced	80.01
Rural Women		
	Unmarried	9.37
	Married	8.12
	Widowed	10.35
	Divorced	16.09
Urban Men		
	Unmarried	35.68
	Married	30.72
	Widowed	102.93
	Divorced	124.63
Urban Women		
	Unmarried	15.05
	Married	9.83
	Widowed	20.49
	Divorced	31.02

Source: Hans Hartelius, "A Study of Suicides in Sweden 1951-63," **Acta Psychiatrica et Neurologica Scandinavica** (Copenhagen), Vol 43 (1967), p. 128.

TABLE 11

Suicide Rates in U.S. per 100,000 Persons 15 Years & Over in Different Marital-status Groups, 1964

Status	Male	Female	Both Sexes
Single	18.2	4.4	12.1
Married	21.1	6.2	13.6
Widowed	74.4	11.1	24.3
Divorced	88.0	20.0	48.0
All Marital-status Groups	24.1	6.9	15.2

Source: **Suicide in the United States 1950-64,** U.S. Dept. of Health, Education, and Welfare, Series 20, Number 5 (Aug., 1967), Table 6.

There is a significant difference in suicide rates between rural and urban areas for both sexes in Sweden (Table 12). In the

TABLE 12

Suicides in Sweden Per 100,000 Persons Over 15 Years of Age, Rural & Urban, 1925-63

Period	Rural		Urban	
	Men	Women	Men	Women
1925-37	31.8	7.5	39.1	8.9
1938-50	27.3	7.4	34.0	11.2
1951-63	33.7	8.8	37.0	13.0

Source: Hans Hartelius, "A Study of Suicides in Sweden 1951-63," . . ., p. 127.

United States the non-metropolitan counties have somewhat higher rates for the sexes combined than metropolitan counties (Table 13). The rates in non-metropolitan counties are higher for men

120   *Deviant Behavior in Sweden*

TABLE 13

Suicides in U.S. per 100,000 population for metropolitan counties and non-metropolitan counties, 1964

Counties	Both Sexes	Male	Female
Metropolitan	10.4	15.7	5.3
Non-metropolitan	10.8	17.6	4.0

Source: **Suicide in the United States 1950-1964,** U.S. Dept. of Health, Education and Welfare, August, 1967, Table 3.

and lower for women than the rates in metropolitan counties. Gibbs states:

> . . . during the 19th century, the urban suicide rates exceeded the rural rate in virtually all countries and provinces. Yet during recent decades the rural-urban difference in rates has changed sharply in some countries. For example, during the period 1904-1913, the urban suicide rate in the United States . . . was 17.7, while the rural rate was only 12.2. Over the decades the rural-urban differences have declined, and . . . by 1960 the rural rate actually was slightly higher.[5]

TABLE 14

Suicides in Sweden by Method, 1956-67

		Poisoning	Hanging	Drowning	Shooting, Blasting	Other Methods
Men	Number	3,736	5,072	992	2,119	909
	Per Cent	29.12	39.53	7.73	16.51	7.08
Women	Number	2,132	993	736	49	452
	Per Cent	48.87	22.76	16.87	1.12	10.36
Total	Number	5,868	6,065	1,728	2,168	1,361
	Per Cent	34.13	35.28	10.05	12.61	7.91

Source: **Statistical Abstract of Sweden, 1968.**

Alcoholism and Suicide

Seventy years ago Durkheim found little or no relationship between the amount of alcohol consumption and suicide. He stated that European countries had varying rates of alcohol consumption but that only Denmark had "both many suicides and a large consumption of alcohol."[6] However, more important than the amount of alcohol consumed is the way it is consumed. If drinking is impulsive so that alcohol is gulped in large amounts and if it is not accompanied by eating or group rituals, drinking may express serious personal problems and may actually be a way of committing suicide.

Dahlgren found that of 96 males who had attempted suicide and had been admitted to the Malmö General Hospital during the years 1933 to 1942, 46, almost half, were inebriates.[7]

In 1955 R. W. Ettlinger and P. Flordh found that of a sample of 500 attempted suicides in a Stockholm hospital, 18.2 per cent were alcoholics.[8]

According to W. A. Rushing, a large body of evidence shows that alcoholism and suicide are rather closely related in various countries. Rushing states that the strongest relationship between alcoholism and suicide exists in groups severely sanctioned for their drinking.[9]

To say that alcoholism sometimes causes suicide is only to push back the casual sequence which needs interpretation. It is necessary to know why men become alcoholics. The onset of alcoholism generally indicates a serious disruption in human relations. Alcoholism constitutes a kind of escape from serious social dilemmas and in itself is more or less a suicidal process. It is not surprising that some alcoholics go all the way to the overt act of suicide.

Mental Illness and Suicide

Durkheim argues that "insanity" can account for relatively few suicides. He states that occasionally there are mental patients who kill themselves to escape imagined danger or disgrace or because they are suffering from extreme oppression and irresistible impulses and obsessions. He insists, however, that the great majority of suicides are not insane and that they have real objective reasons, not imaginary ones, for killing themselves. Because of the long history of stigmatization of suicides, and because suicide seems "contrary to nature," popular opinion has long entertained the idea that only the man who is mentally sick would kill himself. Durkheim, however, maintains that there is no correlation between mental illness and the varying rates of suicides in the various provinces and countries of Europe.[10]

In recent years some psychiatrists and social behaviorists think of functional mental illness as indicative of disturbed social relations. The mentally ill person has a social-adjustment problem similar to that of the alcoholic. Szasz states there are diseases of the brain and nerves, such as paresis and chorea, but that there are no diseases of the "mind" involving organic impairment. To suppose that one is the victim of a widespread communist plot, or that one's body is slowly turning to stone, is a manner of thinking and a way of community communications which indicate problems in living and social adjustments. A disease of the brain is a neurological defect, but the belief in a communist plot against one's job can be explained only on the basis of disturbed human relations. Szasz believes that there is a widespread assumption that human relations are "inherently harmonious" and that disturbance in such relations must be due to mental illness. He says this is fallacious reasoning.[11]

Schizophrenia and acute depressive conditions, which figure most frequently in suicides among the mentally ill, represent forms of retreat from active involvements in life and thus indicate, even as does alcoholism, a kind of beginning of the suicidal process.

Most psychiatrists who make studies of suicides maintain that mental disorder is an important factor. However, there is much variation in the studies concerning the emphasis on mental disorder. In a résumé of studies in various countries the World Health Organization found that studies in some countries ascribed less than 1 per cent of suicides to mental disorder, whereas in some other countries 20 per cent to more than two-thirds of the suicides were thus classified.[12] Gibbs found 34 per cent of all suicides in New Zealand in 1946-51 (955 cases) "may have suffered from some form of mental disorder, a number almost identical with an average of 33 per cent reported in 16 studies of completed and attempted suicide."[13]

Dahlgren states that in Sweden studies by Backlin in 1937 and Alstromin in 1942 "have shown that suicide frequency in mental hospitals, in spite of supervision, and in spite of all other devices and measures to prevent suicide . . . is several times as high as the suicide frequency in the population as a whole."[14]

Dahlgren found that of the 237 cases of attempted suicide admitted to the General Hospital in Malmö, a third were suffering from psychoses. Nineteen were suffering from schizophrenia, 17 from manic-depressive psychosis, 19 from "psychopathia together with the abuse of alcohol," 11 from "other psychopathia," and 30 from "neuroses in hysterical subjects."[15]

Similarly United States data reveal that suicide rates in mental hospitals are several times the rates within the general population. Suicidal tendencies are particularly high among schizophrenics and manic-depressives.[16]

Hospitalization, aside from the suicidal tendencies characterizing the person as he enters, may itself increase tendencies to suicide or even cause them. Hospitalization is often characterized by depersonalization. The individual may be neglected by relatives and friends so that suicide may result from isolation and loneliness rather than from mental illness as such.

INTERPRETATION

The aim of interpretation of suicides is not some kind of ontological explanation of why suicides occur. Rather the purpose is to identify social and psychological factors which may relate to suicide rates. Particularly we are concerned with the question why there has been an increase in suicide rates in Sweden in modern times and why the rate is apparently higher than in most other Western countries.

Climate

The idea that the long, dark winters in Sweden can be blamed for the frequency of suicide can be dismissed at once. The climate has been quite constant from 1785, when the suicide rate was only 2.2 per 100,000 population, to 1967, when the rate was 21.6, an increase of almost 1,000 per cent. It is axiomatic that a constant factor cannot be the cause of a variable factor. Moreover, a country like Norway, which stretches even further to the north, has a suicide rate about half that of Sweden. Bleak Iceland on the Arctic Circle also has a low suicide rate. Denmark has the best climate of the Scandinavian countries but in most years has a suicide rate significantly higher than the rate in Sweden.

Population Factors

Sweden has had relatively low birth rates for several decades. This has created a population with a higher proportion of middle-aged and older people, who everywhere have higher suicide rates than children and young people.

Sweden has not been involved in war since 1815, so that it has no lopsided sex ratio, with a large excess of women in certain age brackets. Since males in all countries have higher suicide rates than females, the sex ratio in Sweden no doubt makes for a slightly higher suicide rate than would otherwise exist. Again, about 20 per cent of the Swedish population never marry, and since single persons have somewhat higher rates than the married, this factor may increase the suicide rates slightly. On the other hand, single persons will never experience widowhood or divorce, statuses with high suicide rates, so that this factor may outbalance the non-marriage factor.

Recording of Suicides

As previously explained, the efficiency of recording suicide statistics may make the rate in Sweden seem higher than it actually is in comparison wth the rate in other countries.

Hendin's Psychiatric Study

In 1964 Hendin, an American psychoanalyst, published a study on suicide in Scandinavia.[17] Using psychoanalytic interview techniques, he sought to explain the relatively high suicide rates of Sweden and Denmark and the relatively low rate of Norway. He interviewed 25 attempted-suicide hospital patients in each country, plus a like number of non-suicidal patients and non-patients, in an attempt to understand the psychodynamics of suicide. Auxiliary aids to this understanding, he believes, are to be found in the literature, popular stories, cartoons, movies, religious beliefs, and the like. Hendin analyzed dreams and life histories of patients in an attempt to understand the motivations for suicide. True to the psychoanalytic tradition, his greatest stress is on the child-parent relationships of the child's earliest years. According to Hendin, these relationships lead to "national character" differences some of which are more conducive to suicide than others.

In Denmark, Hendin found that the principal form of discipline in the family is for the mother to tell the child how hurt she is about the child's misbehavior. She has an extraordinary ability to arouse guilt. From the beginning the mother conditions the child to be highly dependent on her. The child is fondled to a later age than is generally true in the United States. Part of the price which the child pays for his dependence is that his aggressiveness is strictly checked. This in turn tends to increase his dependence.

If there is a breakdown of love or if family relationships are ended by divorce or death, that is, if a "dependency loss" occurs, there is bound to be considerable depression and some vulnerability to suicide. Often there are fantasies about reunion after death with the mother, and others, on whom one has been very dependent. Paradoxically the child's inhibited aggressions may turn on himself and result in suicide.

In Sweden, Hendin "was impressed by the Swedish male patients' preoccupation with performance and success and by the relationship between these concerns and their suicide attempts.

The Swede's ambitiousness and his intensive pursuit of money and material goods seemed as strong as anything seen in the United States. . . ."[18] Danish men, on the other hand, seldom referred to work as a problem but rather centered their anxiety on the loss of a dependency "love object."

Hendin thinks that in Sweden woman is seen as one for whom one must perform well—in childhood with physical development and success in studies at school; in adulthood with methodical work habits and success in the acquisition of status and material goods. In Denmark dependence on the mother is constantly encouraged and cultivated. In Sweden the reverse is true: the child is encouraged early to separate from his mother and learn to perform on his own if he is to receive esteem and parental approval. Swedish mothers push their children of both sexes into an extremely early independence.

The males experience bitterness and anxiety over the child-mother relationships, although they consciously deny it. For females the disturbance is not so disguised and hidden as in the case of men. Upon marriage there are frequent disturbances between husbands and wives, and such disturbances Hendin considers to be a reflection of parental rejection in early childhood.

The child rejected by the mother has anger toward the mother but is taught to keep it under control, to be calm, quiet, and not to cry. Without opportunity to turn his aggression upon others, an immense self-hatred may develop. This is fertile ground for suicide. Thus Hendin thinks suicide rates in Denmark are high because of overdependence of the child on the mother; in Sweden the rates are high because of the tendencies of mothers to push their children into early self-dependence and success. The performance goal is deeply ingrained in childhood through the pressure and expectations of the mother. The child is severely ashamed if he fails. If, as an adult, he does not attain "ambitious goals or rigidly defined standards" his aggressiveness may turn inward, making him vulnerable for suicide.

In Norway, where the suicide rate is low, Hendin found that some patients had overattachments to their mothers. However, the mother's dependency for the child is counterbalanced by her desire for an independent child. At the same time such independence does not mean lack of emotional involvement by the mother as in Sweden. Nor does it set as rigid a demand for the child's successful performance as in Sweden so that lack of achievement does not mean there is need for extreme self-punishment such as suicide.

Norwegians have ways of dealing with aggression, which Hendin thinks is the key factor preventing higher suicide rates. Both children and adults in Norway are expected to express their anger. There is no need to repress it as in Denmark and in Sweden. Norwegians escape the problem of emotional reserve and the retroflexion of anger which is characteristic of the Swedes and an important factor in their suicide rates.

Hendin found Norwegians less involved in a competitive struggle than the Swedes. Norwegians presumably learn to turn their anger outward upon others and upon general situations, thereby dissipating it and preventing a fatal turning in of resentments upon the self.

Although Hendin's analysis offers some clues to national differences in suicide rates, the enlightenment is limited. Twenty-five attempted suicides constitute a very limited sample. Moreover, to attempt suicide may have a different meaning from the suicidal act which succeeds. Although Hendin chose cases which seemed to have made serious attempts at suicide, one cannot be sure that actual suicide was the intent. An attempt at suicide may be nothing more than a plea for attention and help. Dublin states that in the United States there are seven to eight times as many attempts at suicide as there are actual suicides.[19] It is difficult to imagine that if all these persons really wanted to end their lives, they would fail to find the means to do so.

Swedish "national character" probably has some significance for the suicide rate. One wonders, however, why the rate has been changing when the national character of emotional reserve and inhibition of aggressive feelings has apparently existed for some time. Carlsson has pointed to several writers before 1914 who portrayed Swedes as characterized by "emotional dryness and coldness" at a time when suicide rates were appreciably lower.

He thinks that Swedish national character, the reality of which is still only hypothetical, may be "a survival, at least partly, from an earlier epoch of a peasant society under poor farming conditions . . . where the village community was broken up relatively early in many parts of the country [as a result of socio-economic reforms following the breakdown of feudalism.]"[20]

The Psychoanalytic Approach in General

Many psychiatrists continue to lean heavily on Freudian concepts in the interpretation of suicide. Freud believed that man's main goal is happiness. The ideal happiness would be possible only in a kind of Garden of Eden, where a man and a woman could expend their full sexual love on each other with no rival groups or society laying claim for loyalty and friendship, thus subtracting from this love. To Freud love was a total block amount which cannot be expanded, so that when it is expended in one direction, such as love of country, it subtracts from the full sexual love which alone gives pleasure.

Man wants love and happiness, but society stands in the way. Society seeks to combine its members with powerful identifications which, however, exact a heavy toll from the love life of the individual. The individual is under pressure to love his fellow men, but he can actually find only one or, at best, a few toward whom he can feel real love. The others are strangers and are not worthy of love. They do not manifest love toward the individual and actually are worthy only of hostility.

The truth, said Freud, is that there is a powerful desire for aggression against others, a desire which is instinctual and is rooted in the individual's own innate death wish. The individual manages to keep living only as he is able to turn his death wish inside out against others.

If men are deprived of aggression, they are ill at ease. Significant portions of mankind can unite only as long as there are some objects of aggression, such as minority groups or foreign nations. Civilization requires a sacrifice not only of full sexual love and pleasure but also of aggression against others of one's own group or nation.

Sometimes the suicide seeks to kill not only himself but the hated image of someone with whom he has identified himself, so that in killing himself he does not simply vent his anger against himself but turns against a hated object inside himself.

Society can control man's aggressions only in part. It pressures the individual to inhibit his antagonisms, but if he overly internalizes, it will be directed against his ego in the form of a guilty conscience. If the internal aggression becomes a powerful self-hate, he may not be able to resist suicide.[21]

Contemporary psychoanalysts have modified Freud in a variety of ways, placing more emphasis on social and cultural factors and less emphasis on biological factors, such as the innate death wish. However, the changing emphasis has not led to a consistent general theory of suicide. The practice of extensive analysis of individual case studies of suicides is still common, with rather ineffectual attempts to discover common factors for generalizations.

The concept of aggression is still prominent in the analytical systems of psychoanalysts, and they find it particularly useful for the interpretation of suicide. Thus Menninger states that there are three components in any given suicide, namely, the wish to kill, the wish to be killed, and the wish to die.[22] The first involves conscious hate, the second guilt, and the third general hopelessness.

Hartelius states:

> . . . in the final act [of suicide] aggressiveness predominates, and self-destruction is a murder in which the suicide is generally just as much the subject as the object. The perverted aggressiveness . . . is the next main motive force, the suicide then appearing chiefly as the object. A real desire to die, which is not the same as [the desire] to be killed, is more doubtful as a motive force. . . . During a war there is always a free outlet for aggressive abreactions (against the enemy) and the suicide rate invariably falls in wartime (except possibly in total defeat).[23]

It is puzzling why many psychiatrists insist that self-hate and the desire to kill must be present before suicide can take place. It would seem that at least some suicides need not involve a mishandling of aggression. It seems reasonable to suppose that suicide can take place as a rational act by someone who is weary of life or who faces a long and painful terminal illness. Particularly this should be possible in a country with high-level education and with a minimal amount of supernatural controls, like Sweden. Walther T. Martin states that ". . . it is doubtful whether all suicide victims have shown signs of intense emotional or mental disturbance. Indeed, many suicides are carried out in an extremely rational manner."[24]

If suicide is an act of retroflexed aggression, and since persons under 45 are presumably capable of as much aggression as those over 45, why is it that about two-thirds of the suicides in Sweden are over 45?

Psychiatrists tend to see homicide and suicide as two sides of the same coin. It is supposed, therefore, that if a society has a low homicide rate, it necessarily will have a high suicide rate. Since Swedes are a non-violent people with a very low homicide rate, it might therefore be supposed, according to psychiatric logic, that a high suicide rate is to be expected.

However, cross-cultural comparisons fail to support the thesis that homicide and suicide rates are inversely related. Thus Norway has a low suicide rate and also a low homicide rate, while Finland has high rates of both homicide and suicide. In a study of murder and suicide in non-literate societies Palmer found that there was a definite tendency for murder and suicide to vary together rather than inversely.[25]

Sociological Theory

Some important leads for the interpretation of the differing rates of suicide in societies and groups are to be found in sociological theories first enunciated by Emile Durkheim in his book *Suicide,* originally published in 1897.[26]

Durkheim believed that it is fruitless to attempt to explain suicide rates by analyzing the motives of persons who commit suicide or attempt it. The variety of circumstances of individual suicides is almost infinite. There are some who kill themselves because of seemingly slight troubles, whereas others live through great misfortune. In any case motivations are complicated, and it is generally impossible to establish clearly the motivations from suicide notes and the statements of the victims' relatives and associates.

Hence suicides can only be explained socially, that is, by relating suicide rates to the changing conditions in society. Suicide is not strictly an individual act; it takes place in a social environment. Once societal analysis has taken place, one may obtain additional insight through the study of individual suicides, but it is not possible to work the other way around. The social structure, social values, traditions, and typical patterns of social behavior must be understood if suicide rates are to have any meaning.

Crucial factors relating to suicide are changes in society which throw individuals on their own resources. When individuals are firmly rooted in kinship and other community structures, suicide rates tend to be low. When the social structure is dislocated and fragmented so that individuals become, as it were, free-floating atoms, suicide rates are bound to be high. Durkheim applied the term "egoistic" to suicides in such situations.

In line with this general theory, Durkheim found suicide rates generally higher in Protestant countries and provinces than in Catholic areas. Protestants tend to seek more learning and to be on their own with respect to religious beliefs, more so than Catholics, who are generally ensconced within parishes where the pronouncement of "truth" is left to the church hierarchy. Judaism, because of a long history of persecution, has been able to maintain a social cohesion in spite of learning; hence Jews have low suicide rates.

The principle of social cohesion similarly can explain, according to Durkheim, why the married have lower suicide rates than the unmarried and why the larger families have lower rates than small families. The greater density of a family group makes for stronger collective sentiments and reduces excessive individualism. Similarly, rural villages have lower rates than urban areas, because of differential degrees of social cohesion.

Durkheim developed a closely related concept which he called "anomic suicide." A condition of anomie obtains when a rapidly changing society develops not only excessive individualism but also a condition of normlessness. Authoritative standards are weakened so that there is an ineffectual regulation of the way men meet their needs.

Anomic suicide can result from overweening ambitions which are not socially controlled. When rules and restraints weaken, men pursue their goals without social norms to guide them. They may develop desires for an ever-increasing amount of material goods and social prestige—desires which can never really be satisfied. Similarly if controls over sex are weak or non-existent, the individual may search frantically for ever more sex satisfaction, but the more frantic his search the less satisfied he becomes. Once the process of needs-satisfactions is thrown open without social controls, man tends to want ever more and more. Particularly if a person attains sudden wealth and power, he may fail to see the limits of what he can do. His greed has been aroused, but he does not have the knowledge and means of ever satisfying it, and so ends up with disillusionment. He sets unattainable goals, hence is ever unhappy. Only when desires can be limited by a moral regulating force originating in society can satisfactions be maximized.

Durkheim noted that industrial and commercial occupations bring the greatest number of suicides. He believed this to be due to anomic conditions. Conversely, he found agriculture has a relatively low rate of suicide, because the desires of men are more regulated and controlled, not only by society but also by nature.

The concept of anomic suicide and the concept of egoistic suicide are closely interrelated. Both spring from society's deficiency. Egoistic suicide results from society's being deficient in collective activities, whereas anomic suicide results when society provides ineffectual check reins on individual desires. Actually it is hard to imagine either social condition without the other. The general principle, as Durkheim states it, is that "suicide varies inversely with the degree of integration of the social groups of which the individual forms a part."[27]

The rise in the suicide rates in Sweden, Table 8, has correlated with the growth of urbanism and industry. In mid-19th century the rates were only about 6 per 100,000 per year. By 1900, and the early years of the 20th century, the rates had doubled. At the same time urbanism was increasing. Industrialism came relatively late to Sweden, but its impact for social change was heavy when it came. Since 1900 the suicide rate has continued to grow, while industrialism, urbanism, and social and geographic mobility of the population have also continued to increase.

Table 11 indicates that almost two-thirds of the suicides in Sweden are by persons 45 years old and over. Again, the relatively weak relational system, as older people are likely to experience it, comes into play. Older people generally had high social status in earlier traditional society. Family and community ties are less certain and secure in urban-industrial society, so that older people may feel displaced and without status. Some may be alienated and without anchorage in primary social groups. This is particularly true when one member of a married couple has preceded the other in death or when neither has any employment.

Tables 12 and 13 demonstrate how the urban rates of suicide, except for single men, continue to be higher than the rural rates for both men and women. The difference between the urban and rural rates for the widowed and divorced are particularly high. The weak social relational system of urban life accentuates the loneliness of the widowed and the divorced. The strong social controls by tightly knit villages and rural areas are in sharp contrast to the anonymity of urban life. Likewise, alcoholism and mental illness are more likely to make for personal isolation in areas where much anonymity prevails, thereby increasing the vulnerability to suicide. In his study of suicides and attempted suicides in Sweden, Hartelius notes that "there is a definite preponderance of suicides among lonely persons."

There is no way of fully explaining a national suicide rate. The sociological theories of suicide throw light on the problem in a broad way. It may be that there are some intangibles such as "national character," "the way children are brought up," and the "values a society pursues" which make a strategic difference in various individual cases. The broad framework, however, is fairly clear. A society's suicide rate is bound to increase as broad social changes occur—changes which suddenly increase the probabilities that a greater number of individuals will be socially isolated and forced to face more of life's problems on their own resources. Welfare measures should reduce the isolation somewhat, but they scarcely suffice to counterbalance the fracturing forces of modern society.

NOTES

1. Emile Durkheim, *Suicide* (Glencoe, Ill.: Free Press, 1951), p. 50.

2. Louis I. Dublin, *Suicide: A Sociological and Statistical Study* (New York: Ronald Press, 1963), p. 3.

3. Franco Ferracuti, "Suicide in a Catholic Country," in Edwin S. Shneidman & Norman L. Ferracuti, *Clues to Suicide* (New York: McGraw-Hill, 1957).

4. *Acta Psychiatrica et Neurological Scandinavica* (Copenhagen), Vol. 32 (1957), pp. 154 f.

5. Jack P. Gibbs, "Suicide," in Robert K. Merton & Robert A. Nisbet, *Contemporary Social Problems,* 2nd ed. (New York: Harcourt, Brace & World, 1966), pp. 301 f.

6. Durkheim, pp. 78 f.

7. K. G. Dahlgren, *On Suicide and Attempted Suicide* (Lund, Sweden: Lindstedt's University Bokhandel, 1945), p. 145.

8. World Health Organization, *Prevention of Suicide* (Geneva, 1968), p. 66.

9. "Suicide and the Interaction of Alcohol," Part B, *Quarterly Journal of Studies on Alcohol,* Vol. 29, No. 4 (Dec., 1968), pp. 988 ff.

10. Durkheim, pp. 57-77.

11. Thomas Szasz, "The Myth of Mental Illness," in Harry Silverstein, *The Social Control of Mental Illness,* (New York: Crowell, 1968).

12. World Health Organization, pp. 61 f.

13. Gibbs, pp. 299 f.

14. Dahlgren, p. 79.

15. *Ibid.,* p. 86.

16. Dublin, pp. 170-72.

17. Herbert Hendin, *Suicide and Scandinavia* (New York: Grune & Stratton, 1964).

18. *Ibid.,* p. 44.

19. Dublin, p. 3.

20. Gösta Carlsson, "Swedish Character in the Twentieth Century," *Annals of the American Academy*, No. 370 (Mar., 1967), pp. 93-98.

21. This brief statement is based most directly on Freud's *Civilization and Its Discontents*.

22. Karl Menninger, *Man Against Himself* (New York: Harcourt, Brace, 1938), pp. 24-80.

23. Hans Hartelius, "A Study of Suicides in Sweden, 1925-1950," *Acta Psychiatrica et Neurologica Scandinavica*, Vol. 43 (1967), p. 169.

24. "Theories of Variation in the Suicide Rate," in Jack P. Gibbs, ed., *Suicide* (New York: Harper & Row, 1968), p. 92.

25. Stuart Palmer, "Murder and Suicide in Forty Nonliterate Societies," *Journal of Criminal Law, Criminology and Police Science*, Vol. 56 (Sept., 1965), pp. 320-24.

26. Durkheim.

27. *Ibid.*, p. 209.

VII

Sexual Norms and Sexual Deviance

Discussion of sex in Sweden is frank and open. There is little or no reticence in exploring the meaning of sex in the press, movies, group sessions, or the schools. Sex can be discussed in great detail without embarrassment. For example, there is an ongoing debate over whether sex relations for younger adolescents can be socially approved or whether society ought to discourage "instant sex" between persons who are strangers or only casually acquainted.

There was candid talk about the use of contraceptives for adolescents in a group meeting of mothers of young teenage daughters. The women were agreed that schools should teach adolescents how to use contraceptives. They believed that the open availability of contraceptives in vendo-mats on the streets and other public places was a good thing. When asked if this would mean a greater probability of sexual involvements for their daughters, the women readily approved of contraceptives for their girls, for, as one said, "Our girls will have sex relations in any case, and they ought to know how to guard themselves against pregnancies and disease." Several stated that as mothers they would always be concerned, not about whether their daughters had sex relations but about the type of boys with whom they would have such relations. Only if the girls associated with "the wrong type of boys" should they need to have any guilt feelings about sex relations. "If no coercion or seduction is involved," one woman said, "there is no reason why a girl should feel guilty about sex." When I stated that the bishops of the state church had condemned premarital sex relations, one woman said she did not know what the bishops had said but that in any case it did not matter, since "the church is no longer relevant to modern life." The women seemed agreed that sex experience before marriage is "generally a good thing because it makes for better marriages." One of them summarized it, "As with everything else, it is experience that counts."

Sex is not shrouded in shame or fear. Nudity is not shameful; it is said that embarrassment over bodily exposure between parents and children is rare. There are those who enjoy sunning themselves in the nude, although this is generally done in sheltered areas between buildings, on rooftops, or on private beaches.

It is not necessary to disguise travel by unmarried couples. An Uppsala coed told freely of her foreign travels with a male friend. There is nothing unusual about such arrangements.

The Swedes pride themselves on being practical. Jenkins characterizes the Swedish attitude toward sex, "Since the sexual instinct appears to be ineradicable, the Swedes reason that the problem is, not how to suppress it, but how to organize it as efficiently as possible."[1]

PREMARITAL SEX RELATIONS

In Sweden's rural past, as in other Scandinavian countries, there was considerable sex permissiveness for young courting couples and those engaged to be married. For hundreds of years the rules of courtship, although frowning upon general promiscuity, allowed a young man to sleep with his fiancée. Frequently wedding arrangements were not made until the girl became pregnant or gave birth to a child. Long before the time of the wedding, the parental families of the couple had given their approval so that a socially sanctioned marriage could be said to exist, though it lacked legal and religious sanction until the rites were said.[2]

Today sex relations between those who are "going steady" or who are engaged to be married continues to be taken for granted, with very little opposition or criticism. Carl-Gustave Boethius, editor of the *Church of Sweden* magazine, recently told a news conference that "two-thirds of Swedish women are pregnant before they marry and 95 per cent have sexual relations before marriage."[3] Fleisher states that "today, 43 per cent of the brides in the country are pregnant on their wedding day and over 80 per cent of the brides and grooms have had premarital relations."[4]

Studies of Premarital Sex Behavior

In a study carried out by the official Youth Committee in the 1940's and reported by Kalvesten, a high frequency of premarital relations was recorded. Among the males with only grade-school training, 95 per cent said they had experienced premarital relations. Young men with higher education "partly followed another pattern" involving somewhat less experience with premarital relations.[5] Kalvesten reports two other studies of the 1940's. In one case 500 20-year-old single men in military service were interviewed. It was found that "40 per cent of the 'higher education' and 80 per cent of those with only elementary and 'middle-school' training had experienced intercourse." The other study found that "80 per cent of the married women had had intercourse before marriage." Kalvesten does not indicate the size and nature of the sample.[6]

Professor Joachim Israel, of the sociology staff of the University of Uppsala, has made a study of 436 military draftees, 90 per cent of whom were 20 years old. Of these single men, 83 per cent said they had experienced premarital sex relations, 10 per cent refused to answer, and 7 per cent said they had never had sexual relations. The median age of first coitus was below 16 years.[7] Professor Israel is currently engaged in a thorough study of both sex attitudes and sex behavior of 1,300 single youths in Stockholm. He reported to me that of the 1,300 there were only three persons who had not experienced sex relations.

Two studies by Professor Georg Karlsson of the University of Uppsala conducted in 1960 and in 1965 lend support to the belief that the amount of premarital sex relations is increasing.[8] Linner summarizes the study as follows:

> Questions about sex habits were put to students at four People's colleges, where the average student age fluctuated annually between 17 and 23.7. The percentage of students who had experienced intercourse increased from 72 per cent in 1960 to 81 per cent in 1965. The rise among girls was especially pronounced, from 40 per cent to 65 per cent. Even more striking was the increase at church-affiliated schools: from 37.8 per cent to 76.9 per cent. One such school registered the highest figures in both

surveys. In 1960, 79.5 per cent had had intercourse, while in 1965, as many as 86.9 per cent had. Even among those students who had attended a church service at least twelve times during the past year, the results were similar: 53.7 per cent of the 1965 survey said they had experienced coitus, as against 37.3 per cent in 1960. The median age at first coitus for boys fell from 18 years in 1960 to 17 in 1965. For girls, it dropped from 18 to 17.6.

A current study, sponsored by a Royal Commission of Sweden and carried out by Professor Hans L. Zetterberg of Ohio State University, is based on a representative sample of 1,952 Swedes. It finds that the young begin sex relations somewhat earlier than had the parents. The young also have more sexual partners than older persons. Thus "for men above 30 years, the mean is seven sex partners; for younger men (21 to 30), with fewer years for sex relations, the mean is already eight."[9]

Zetterberg found that between 1920 and 1950 the age for the beginning of sex relations declined a year and that this decline is continuing. Sex activity is not a mere brief interlude; once begun, it tends to continue. The educated begin their sex somewhat later but "eventually catch up and have more sex partners than the less educated." Ninety-three per cent of the sample approved of sex relations between those going steady and those who are engaged. Ninety-eight per cent of the married persons in the sample had sex relations before marriage.[10]

Casual Sex

Premarital sex relations are changing not only in that there is a growing rate of such relations but also in that a larger percentage of sex relations are apparently of a more casual type than heretofore. Zetterberg found, however, that ". . . the constancy of a good relationship is respected." The new morality does not "generate a free-for-all."

In the history of Western societies there has generally been greater permissiveness for young men than for young women. However, as women have gained more equality, and since prostitution in Sweden has virtually disappeared, the behavior of the two sexes is becoming more similar.

Some remnants of the double standard persist. Zetterberg found that "the majority of men have had as many as five sex partners, while the majority of women, only one or two. . . . More persons would permit men to have premarital experience than women. And more women accept the idea of a double standard than do men."[11]

I interviewed some sex-education teachers in secondary schools. After one had explained that she was teaching not only the biology of sex but also the ethics of sex behavior and the use of contraceptives, I asked if the use of birth-control techniques would possibly lead to more casual sexual relations among the young. She explained that premarital sex relations take place mostly between "persons who have deep feelings for each other." When asked if possibly with city living and large variety of social contacts, there may be an increasing number of sex relations between persons who are only casually acquainted, she replied, "No, that is not Sweden's way. Most sex relations take place between persons who are in love and who perhaps plan to be married."

A graduate student in criminology commented on this point of view:

> There are far more premarital relations of the casual variety than those which involve deep feelings of love. It is easy for the adolescent to think he is deeply in love and that sex relations in a given instance express such love. However, we know that emotions are changeable and that an individual may have "deep feelings" with one person one week and with another person the next week. I think that casual sex relations far outnumber the sex relations between serious lovers and that this is true not only for the lower classes but for the middle and upper classes as well.

At least one study supports this point of view. Kalvesten reports that of a group of 500 men none had his first intercourse with a girl who later became his wife; 7 per cent had first relations with a "fiancée," 35 per cent with "a steady girl friend," and 58 per cent with "a casual acquaintance."

This, however, is not to say that general promiscuity prevails. Except for the *raggare* of the larger cities, most of the casual sex relations referred to above generally involve a degree of acquaintance and perhaps a few dates. With the exception of the *raggare*, there is no evidence that boys and girls openly solicit on the streets or in other public places. Most Swedish young people are far too sophisticated and proud for the behavior that open solicitation implies.

But some promiscuity exists in Sweden, as it does in all countries. Promiscuity and "instant sex" are most closely exemplified by the *raggare*, a minority among the youth of Sweden. These youth are restless and rebellious against most adult norms. The *raggare* are the urban teenage hot-rodders. It has been estimated that "perhaps 10 per cent of Swedish teenagers live an undisciplined and unsettled life. . . ."[12] The following from Connery describes a "mating ritual" not too different from what can be observed in many American towns and cities:

> In Stockholm there is a kind of teen-age demimonde. . . . The well-publicized raggare are the most visible of all. They cruise in packs of unmuffled cars, usually flashy secondhand American models, and pick up girls in a modern mating ritual worthy of serious anthropological attention. Minor-league versions of the same exercise can be seen in other Swedish cities. . . . [The cars] move slowly in parade down Kungsgatan, the Broadway of Stockholm, at about the time the cinemas, restaurants and dance halls empty out. The sallow-looking young drivers and their friends, never smiling, never eager, look over the girls drifting along on the sidewalk. A toe touches an accelerator and an unmuffled exhaust pipe emits a deep burbling sound. A girl, or two or three girls, respond to the call by opening the rear door of the car and tumbling into the back seat. The car cuts out of the procession and careens into the night.[13]

The object of the game is "instant sex." The promiscuous male, in these instances, is more or less excused for his behavior. The promiscuous girl is more likely to be criticized. The girl is not expected to be a virgin at marriage. On the other hand, she should not distribute her sexual favors too freely; she is expected to confine her sex relations to going steady or serious love relationships.

Most premarital sex relations in Sweden can scarcely be labeled as deviant behavior. Such relations are widely accepted,

and have been so for a long time, especially when they are between courting couples planning to marry. Only slightly less acceptable are sex relations between friends, acquaintances, or those
dating steady. Least acceptable and qualifying more definitely as
deviant behavior are sex relations between strangers on a pickup
basis.

American Premarital Sex Studies—Compared

It is difficult to make meaningful comparisons between premarital sex behavior in the United States and in Sweden. The two
countries have different historical backgrounds, and the composi-
tion of the United States population is far more heterogeneous.

Kinsey and associates found that about 50 per cent of the
American women in a sample of 8,000 had experienced premarital
coitus while 90 per cent of a sample of 12,000 men had experienced premarital coitus.[14]

The Kinsey study found that the premarital sexual experience
of females was restricted to relatively few sexual partners and, in
many cases, restricted to relatively short periods. Generalizing
about the Kinsey study and three other American studies, Bell
states that "from one-half to two-thirds of the females in their
studies reported premarital coitus only with the men they eventually married."[15]

Forty-four per cent of the females in the Kinsey study stated
that their premarital sex experience was limited to a period of
one year or less. "For nearly a third, the coitus had extended over
a period of two or three years, and for 26 per cent it had extended
over four or more years. However, only a very few females had
had premarital coitus with any continuity over such periods of
time."[16]

The females in the Kinsey studies, especially those of middle
and upper classes, were less promiscuous than the males.

After surveying the available evidence from a variety of premarital sex behavior studies, Bell concludes that ". . . it appears
that the greatest changes in premarital coitus for the American
female occurred in the period around World War I and during

the 1920's. There is no evidence that the rates since that period have undergone any significant change. . . ."[17]

In general, it is evident that premarital sex relations are considerably more widespread and, once begun, more continuous in Sweden than in the United States. Premarital relations of American women are evidently more restricted to men they later marry, while Swedish women are more likely to have relations with several partners.

Premarital Sex and Guilt Feelings

The presence or absence of guilt feelings among those who participate in premarital sex relations gives some indication of the extent to which such behavior is socially approved in a given society. Guilt feelings are hard to gauge and even more difficult to compare between two societies such as the United States and Sweden.

It seems likely that in Sweden, premarital sex relations between those engaged to be married, or even between those "going steady," entail little regret or guilt. Except for an occasional denouncement of all premarital sex relations by the church bishops and a minority of ministers, there is widespread social approval of such relations. Since premarital sex relations between the betrothed have been widely approved in some social classes for hundreds of years in Sweden, they cannot be labeled as deviant behavior leading to guilt and punishment.

There is less certainty of public approval of the more casual type of premarital sex behavior in Sweden. Several sex education teachers in the 7th-, 8th-, and 9th-grade levels said they try to discourage casual sex relations. In fact, one of the main thrusts of the compulsory sex-education program in the schools of Sweden is the emphasis on responsible behavior. Seduction and coercion in sex behavior are condemned. There should be mutuality, social respect, and love between the participants in the sex act and they must have their eyes wide open to the possibility of pregnancy. A happy-go-lucky approach with sex on an exploitive or promiscuous basis is considered unethical.

A number of middle-aged adults whom I interviewed echoed

the same point of view. A few accused youth of being obsessed with sex; one man, a civil engineer, said "the young people are up to their ears in sex." In view of such sentiments among some adults and in view of the emphasis on responsible behavior in sex education, it seems likely that many adolescents would feel some guilt when their sex relations were on a furtive and semi-promiscuous basis.

However, I have not heard any expression of such feelings of guilt. Typically teenagers deny that guilt feelings are ever involved, and teachers and parents often say that the young do not suffer from guilt feelings. A minister of the Church of Sweden, stationed at the University of Uppsala, said, "They are all doing it at about age 15 or 16 and they seem to have no guilt about it. I am more or less against premarital relations and have sometimes said so, but students keep telling me that most other ministers approve."

The Kinsey study of female sex behavior in the United States found that

> Seventy-seven per cent of the married females, looking back from the vantage point of their more mature experience, saw no reason to regret their premarital coitus. Another 12 per cent of the married females had some minor regret.[18]

Bell cites several studies in which the conclusions are similar to those of Kinsey, namely, that the women with premarital sex relations experienced relatively little guilt feeling.[18]

Reiss has recently made an intensive study of premarital behavior and sex attitudes among 1,003 college students, 216 high-school students, and a national sample of 1,515 adults. He found that guilt feelings play an important role in sex behavior. Of the unmarried respondents in a midwestern college sample of 316 persons who were currently adherents to the "petting standard," 55 per cent stated they felt guilty about petting; and 49 per cent of the unmarried who were current adherents to the "coitus standard" felt guilt about it.[20]

However, ". . . three out of every four females [in the midwestern college sample] continue to engage in behavior that makes them feel guilty, and almost nine out of every ten of these eventually come to accept it."[21] Reiss believes that the fact that most previous studies report only a negligible amount of guilt feelings can be explained by the

> . . . differences in the nature of the samples used. An older group of females might well have stabilized their sexual behavior and attitudes so that they had largely resolved what guilt they formerly felt. Kinsey's female respondent's were often older and married, and this may account for their low percentages of "regrets."[22]

A study by Christensen and Carpenter found that both the females and the males in a Danish sample of students gave approval of premarital coitus beyond the amount of coitus they actually experienced, whereas in the other two student samples (one, the "Intermountain," predominantly Mormon background from Utah and the other the "Midwestern" from Indiana) individuals participated in more coitus than what they approved. See Figure 2. The authors surmise that ". . . where there has been premarital coitus by more people than approve, some of these will be harboring guilt feelings about their behavior." On this assumption the Intermountain students must experience the most guilt about their behavior, with the midwestern students ranging in between the Danish and Intermountain but much closer to the Intermountain than the Danish in behavior and guilt.

The authors think that the sexual norms and behavior in Denmark are "broadly typical of all of Scandinavia."[23]

In the above-quoted study, and several others, Harold T. Christensen and associates have found that, as compared with American students, Danish students (1) "give greater approval to both premarital coitus and postmarital infidelity"; (2) approve "earlier starting times, in relation to marriage, of each level of intimacy—necking, petting, and coitus"; (3) think "in terms of a more rapid progression in intimacy development from its beginnings in necking and its completion in coitus."[24]

FIGURE 2

Comparisons of Approval with Experience in Premarital Coitus, College Students

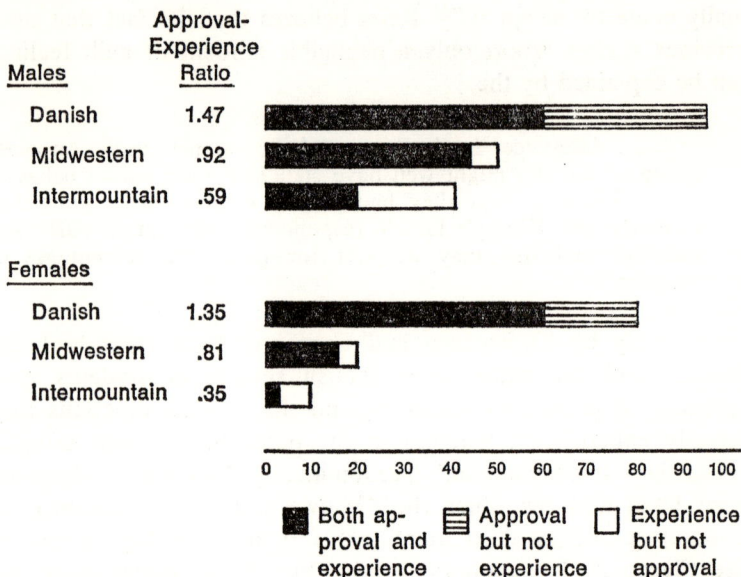

Males	Approval-Experience Ratio
Danish	1.47
Midwestern	.92
Intermountain	.59
Females	
Danish	1.35
Midwestern	.81
Intermountain	.35

Both approval and experience   Approval but not experience   Experience but not approval

Source: Harold T. Christenson & George R. Carpenter, "Value-Behavior Discrepancies Regarding Premarital Coitus in Three Western Cultures," **American Sociological Review,** Vol. 27, No. 1 (Feb., 1962), pp. 66-74. Used by permission.

It is probable that the Danish premarital sex norms and behavior are similar to the Swedish, but the studies by Christensen and associates are hard to compare with Swedish studies of premarital sex behavior because of differences in study design and in the nature of the samples. In Denmark the sample was made up altogether of university students, whereas the samples in several of the Swedish studies consisted of military draftees and of random selections from the youth population.

It is probable, however, that if a group of Swedes were directly compared with a similar group of Americans, the nature of the sex norms and of the behavior would reveal substantive differences, including, for the American subjects, a greater amount of guilt feelings about premarital sex.

SEX OFFENSES AND SEX PROBLEMS

Every society defines some kinds of sexual behavior as offenses against the law. The nature of official permissiveness or rigidity concerning sex behavior probably constitutes a rather significant index of the values of a society as a whole. In this section we consider some categories of sex behavior which have some involvement with the laws and/or are subjects of public controversy.

Prostitution

Prostitution, as such, is not a crime in Sweden. If a woman wants to exchange sexual favors for money or gifts, this is considered her own affair as long as she is not abused in the process or becomes a general public nuisance. Police pick up prostitutes on vagancy charges or because of alcoholism or drug addiction.

Acting as a pimp for prostitutes is against the law. There is also a law which makes it a crime for a person to have "sexual intercourse with a child under fifteen years of age." The Swedish *Penal Code* also states: "A person, who by promising or giving compensation, obtains or tries to obtain a temporary sexual relationship with someone under eighteen years of age or, if he is of the same sex, under twenty-one years, shall be sentenced for seduction of youth to pay a fine or to imprisonment for at most six months."[25]

Prostitution is declining and is not a significant problem in Sweden. There are no licensed houses of prostitution. The customers are said to be mostly middle-aged and older men, rarely teenagers or young men.

The women's rights movement is proclaiming equal rights for women in all things—including the right of women to initiate sex relations. What is right or wrong for men is also right or wrong for women. A man, for example, has no right to go to a prostitute while his wife or fiancée sits at home.

Homosexuality

The *Penal Code* of Sweden states that "if a person who is over
18 years of age has sexual relations with someone of the same
sex who is under 18 . . . he shall be sentenced for carnal abuse
of youth. . . ." There are no laws which forbid homosexual relations between consenting adults, and it would be hard to find
a responsible person in Sweden who advocated such a law.

This does not mean that most Swedes approve of homosexuality. Rather, they see it as one of the unfortunate facts of life
which cannot be suppressed by defining it as criminal. They find
it is better to try to keep it in its place than to make it a crime.
There is no public harassment of homosexuals as long as the
relationships involve only consenting adults in private. Harassment by the law under such circumstances is interpreted as an unwarranted invasion of private life.

Homosexuality, both male and female, is portrayed openly in
a wide variety of magazines displayed on newsstands.

I was told by one movie critic that movie censorship in Sweden
is not generally concerned about sex scenes and sex perversions
unless they involve cruelty and sadism and that in general there is
more censorship of violence than of sex behavior. The Swedes
cannot understand why Americans permit so much violence in
their movies, and the Americans cannot understand why the
Swedes permit so much sex in their movies.

Pornography

Within the last few years large amounts of pornography have
made their appearance on the newsstands and in shops. No doubt
there has always been a certain amount of pornography available
in the cities and towns of Sweden, even as in the United States.
However, as a number of persons explained to me, in the past
there was never the abundance and openness of pornographic
materials there is at present. The pornographic magazines not only
portray nudes in every conceivable pose and heterosexual relations; they also display all the perversions. In fact, the perversions

seem to receive the greater emphasis. One citizen opined that "apparently people are tired of straight nudes and sex pictures and so they seek thrill in bizarre perversions."

Swedes seem at a loss to explain why so much pornography has come on the scene. A sex-education instructor said, "We are embarrassed and disgusted with it. We think it is mostly the older men rather than young people who are buying it."

Since pornography is nearly always directed at men, recently a crusader for women's rights started a pornographic magazine for women with photos of nude men.

The problem of pornography was discussed by some eminent men in the government. They decided that censorship would be a worse evil than the pornography itself. They concluded that in any case, pornography does not do as much harm as some people imagine and that it is wrong to deprive individuals who need it or want it and who perhaps have no other source of sex satisfactions. Others may lose interest in it eventually, and the pornography market will decline.

Pornographic materials have long been available in the United States on a covert, under-the-counter basis in back-street shops. Within the last ten years or so pornography has become much more abundant and more easily available, although it is not displayed as openly as in Sweden. A news story recently declared:

> . . . pornography is big business in America. . . . About 200 companies in the country produce pornographic books, magazines and films. Their works flood millions of American mailboxes, through a chain of distributors, onto the shelves of bookstores across the country.
> Total sales of pornographic material are estimated upward from $500 million a year, dwarfing the likes of the huge Government Printing Office (17 million dollars annual sales).[26]

Illegitimate Births

In 1967 there were 121,360 live births in Sweden. Of these, 103,037 were legitimate and 18,323, or 15 per cent, were illegitimate.[27] In 1957, 10 per cent of all births were illegitimate. It may be noted from Table 15 that the illegitimacy rate in Sweden since

1900 has ranged between about 10 and 16 per cent most of the time. The rates of illegitimacy have been somewhat lower in recent years than in the 1920's and early 1930's. It is obvious that the relatively high rate of illegitimacy is rooted in Sweden's past and cannot be said to be a correlate of modern affluence and state welfarism. The rates at the turn of the 20th century, for example, were not significantly different from the rates of more recent years.

Illegitimacy in Sweden has a very different social meaning than it does in the United States. Every effort is made to avoid labeling a child as illegitimate. Zetterberg recently found that 99 per cent of the Swedish population feels that "children of illegitimate birth should have all the rights of those of legitimate birth."[28] A child born out of wedlock is assigned a child-care supervisor who assists the mother and protects the rights of the child. The father must contribute economic assistance, or if this is impossible, the mother receives financial aid from the government. The mother is encouraged to keep her child, and the majority of the women do keep their children. However, careful procedures for adoption into desirable homes are available should the mother prefer not to keep the child. Every effort is made to make certain the child has the same legal rights and opportunities as other children. There is no evidence that having an illegitimate child is considered a shameful thing. Although a few "forced marriages" occur, the emphasis on the necessity of covering the "shame" of an illegitimate pregnancy with a hasty marriage is far less strong than in the United States.

Table 15 shows the illegitimacy rates in Sweden since 1900. It should be noted that the rates since the development of the welfare state average lower than the rates of the 1920's and 1930's. The evidence does not support the notion, often expressed by critics, that welfare measures increase the amount of illegitimacy. The welfare state has, however, produced an attitude toward the mother and her illegitimate child which is far more moral than the American attitude, which is highly non-humanitarian.

Table 16 shows the illegitimacy rates for the United States, 1940-1965. Figure 3 compares the rates for Sweden and United States to the extent that data for the same years are available.

TABLE 15

Illegitimate Live Births as Per Cent of All Live Births in Sweden, 1900-67

Year	Per Cent Illegitimate Births	Year	Per Cent Illegitimate Births	Year	Per Cent Illegitimate Births
		1928	15.93	1948	9.40
		1929	16.20	1949	9.38
		1930	16.35	1950	9.75
		1931	16.31	1951	10.07
		1932	15.95	1952	9.92
		1933	15.48	1953	9.76
		1934	14.44	1954	9.78
		1935	14.22	1955	9.94
		1936	13.36	1956	No data given
		1937	12.93	1957	10.12
		1938	12.73	1958	10.23
		1939	12.37	1959	10.41
		1940	11.76	1960	11.28
		1941	10.86	1961	11.68
1900	10.86	1942	9.22	1962	12.39
1910	12.71	1943	8.80	1963	12.55
1920	15.01	1944	9.05	1964	13.13
1925	15.15	1945	9.58	1965	13.80
1926	15.38	1946	9.33	1966	14.56
1927	16.03	1947	9.38	1967	15.09

Sources: Data for 1900 through 1950 calculated from Table B10, **Historical Statistics of Sweden: Vital Statistics;** data for 1951 through 1955 calculated from Table 50, **Statistical Abstract of Sweden, 1957;** data for 1957 through 1967 computed from Table 42, **Statistical Abstract of Sweden, 1968.**

TABLE 16

Illegitimate Live Births as Per Cent of All Live Births in United States, 1940-65

Year	Per Cent Illegitimate Births	Year	Per Cent Illegitimate Births
1940	3.8	1955	4.5
1941	3.8	1956	4.6
1942	3.4	1957	4.7
1943	3.3	1958	5.0
1944	3.8	1959	5.2
1945	4.3	1960	5.3
1946	3.8	1961	5.6
1947	3.6	1962	5.9
1948	3.7	1963	6.3
1949	3.7	1964	6.8
1950	4.0	1965	7.7
1951	3.9	1966	8.4
1952	3.9	1967	9.0
1953	4.1	1968	9.7
1954	4.4		

Sources: 1940-65 computed from Table D of **Trends in Illegitimacy,** United States, U.S. Department of Health, Education, and Welfare, Series 21, No. 15; 1966-68 from **Vital Statistics of the U.S.**

It is difficult to compare the illegitimacy rates of Sweden with those of the United States.

"Trends in the illegitimacy rate for the United States are available for a relatively short period of time, because all states were not included in the birth-registration area until 1933 and estimates for the states not reporting illegitimacy were not made until 1938."[29] A comparison is made by the Department of Health, Education, and Welfare with the historical rates in England, where the data go back to 1850 and where the illegitimacy rates in 1850-60 were as high as in 1960. From the early high level, however, the rates gradually declined to low levels in the 1930's and returned by 1960 to the approximate level of 1850-60. During the recorded period in the United States the rates of illegitimacy have been similar to those of England, with a rapid

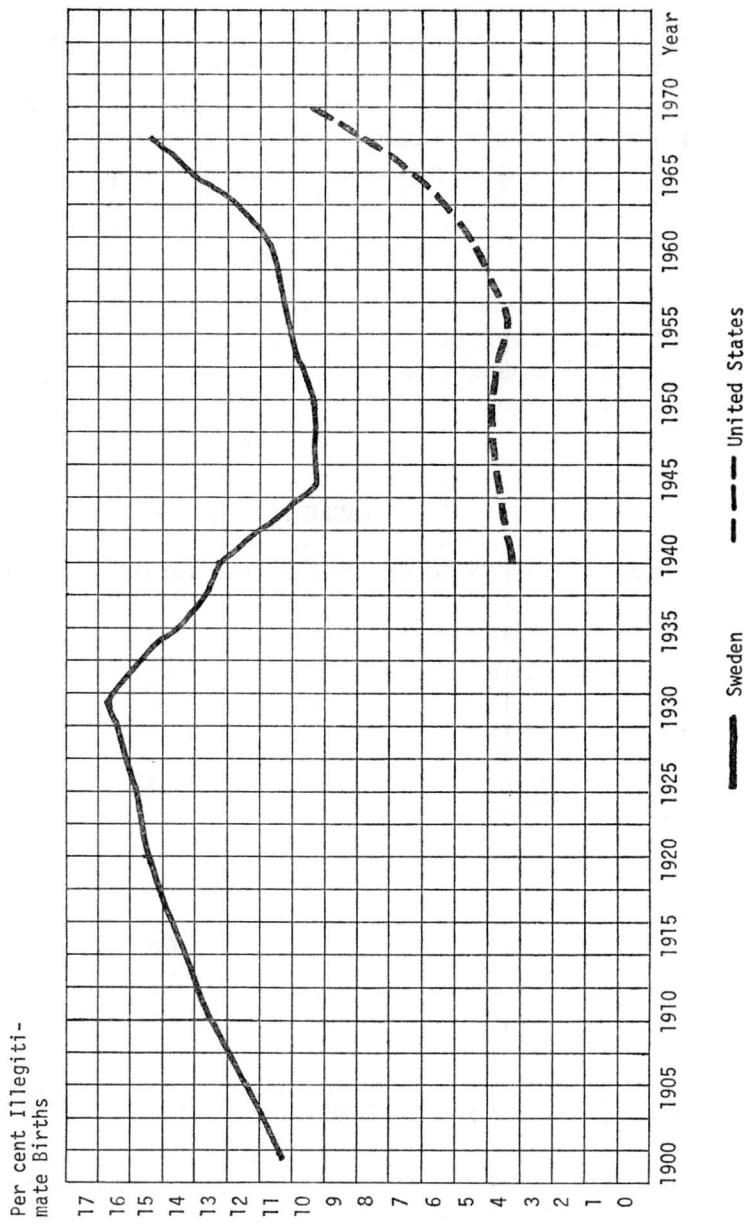

Illegitimate Births as Per Cent of Total Live Births in Sweden and in the United States. (Based on Tables 15 and 16 above.)

Per cent Illegiti-
mate Births

─── Sweden   ─ ─ ─ United States

rise since 1940. This suggests to the United States Department of Health, Education, and Welfare that the "illegitimacy [rate] may have been nearly as high in the past as it is now. In any case, we cannot assume that the currently high rates represent a phenomenon entirely without precedent in Western society."[30]

Venereal Disease

"If there is a truly pessimistic aspect of sex in Swedish society," says Birgitta Linner, "it is the rising frequency of venereal infection. Both gonorrhea and syphilis claim a growing number of victims each year, especially in the fifteen-to-nineteen-year-old age group."[31]

TABLE 17

Syphilis Rates in Sweden, 1920-66, Per 100,000 Population*

Year	Rate	Year	Rate
1941	4.61	1955	2.4
1942	7.03	1956	1.6
1943	15.00	1957	no data
1944	21.09	1958	1.0
1945	21.65	1959	1.3
1946	21.64	1960	1.2
1947	20.54	1961	1.6
1948	16.13	1962	3.3
1949	11.80	1963	4.4
1950	8.90	1964	6.3
1951	6.7	1965	6.3
1952	4.9	1966	5.5
1953	2.7	1967	4.3
1954	2.4	1968	3.4

* Rates are based on number of cases reported during respective years; both congenital and acquired cases are included.

Sources: 1920-50 computed from **Historical Statistics of Sweden,** Table 145; 1951-56 computed from **Statistical Abstract of Sweden** 1967; 1958-67 computed from **Statistical Abstract of Sweden 1968.**

In 1958 there were 77 cases of syphilis in Sweden. In 1967 the number of cases had risen to 499, an increase of 500 per cent in nine years' time. In 1958 there were 12,996 cases of acute gonorrhea, but by 1967 there had been a 100 per cent increase, with 26,024 cases.[32]

TABLE 18

Syphilis Rates in United States, 1941-67, Per 100,000 Population*

Year	Rate	Year	Rate
1941	94.9	1955	16.3
1942	98.7	1956	15.1
1943	121.0	1957	14.3
1944	98.7	1958	12.3
1945	81.5	1959	12.8
1946	84.8	1960	11.8
1947	83.2	1961	12.8
1948	75.7	1962	12.8
1949	66.1	1963	12.0
1950	51.5	1964	11.3
1951	42.2	1965	10.6
1952	30.3	1966	10.3
1953	25.2	1967	9.3
1954	19.8		

* Rates are based on number of cases reported during respective years; both congenital and acquired cases are included.
Source: **Venereal Disease Fact Sheet—1967**, U.S. Dept. of Health, Education, and Welfare, Table 4.

Table 17 shows the incidence rate of syphilis in Sweden since 1920. The trend was downward to 1958. Since then the rate has increased. Table 18 shows the rate of syphilis in the United States. In 1941 the American rate was about 20 times as high as the Swedish rate in the same year. The American rate declined to a low point in 1957 and 1958 but has since increased. In 1967 the American rate was about twice as high as the Swedish rate. The rates are compared in Figure 4.

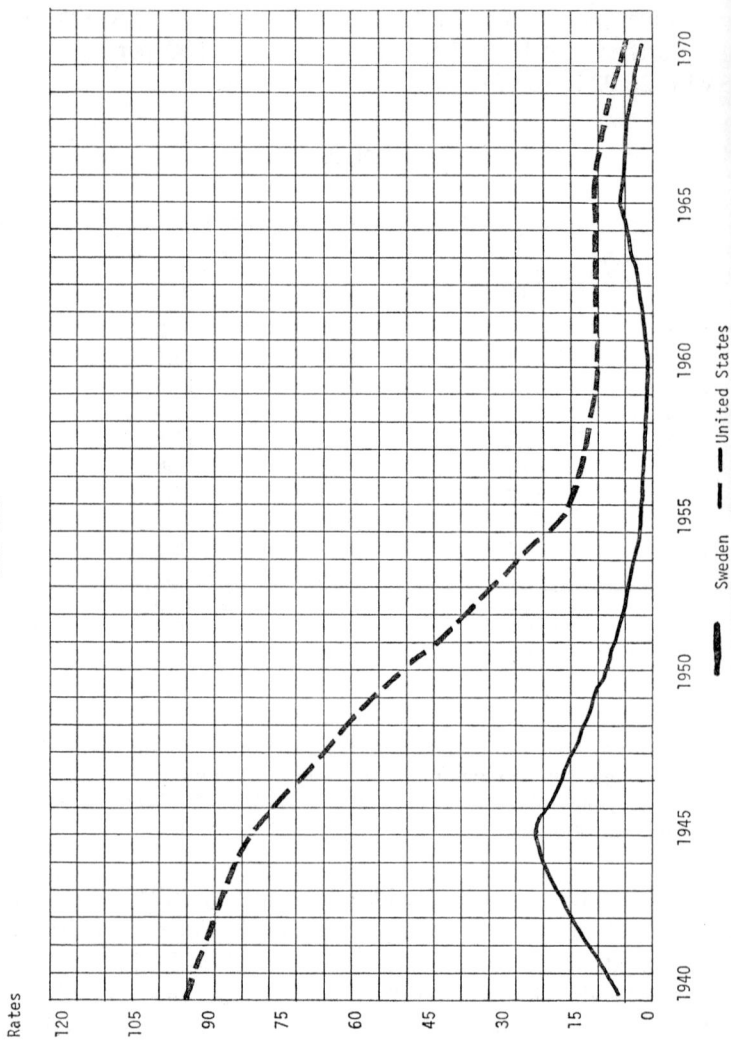

Figure 4
Rates of Syphilis Per 100,000
Population for Given Years
Sweden and the United States
1920-1966

Statistics on the rates of syphilis in the United States and in Sweden must be interpreted with caution. The data are based on the number of cases reported, and we do not know what percentage of the cases is reported. It is probable that a higher percentage of the total cases of syphilis in Sweden is reported than in the United States. This assumption is based on Sweden's having had ten years of compulsory sex education in the schools, where venereal diseases are described and youth are warned to report to a clinic when infection has occurred. Sweden has a much smaller and more homogeneous population than the United States; there are no vast city ghettos where medical services are scarce. Even so, there is no way of knowing what percentage of all cases is reported.

In the United States the fifty states and the District of Columbia reported 21,090 diagnosed cases for 1967. However, "the Venereal Disease Program currently estimates that the actual occurrence of syphilis was about 80,000 cases in . . . 1967. . . . Cases of syphilis which occur but go untreated cumulate to form a large reservoir of cases needing treatment. This reservoir of cases needing treatment (prevalence), most of which are in the latent stage of disease and are detectable only by means of blood tests, is currently estimated to number about 639,000."[33]

What discourages the Swedish health authorities and the instructors in sex education is that the increase in venereal diseases has taken place in spite of first-rate medical care, the virtual absence of prostitution, and careful instruction about venereal diseases in the schools. The National Board of Health brochures advise against "casual sex relations," to consult a doctor at once "if infection has taken place" and to "use a condom" as a reasonably good defense against infection. Contraceptives are sold in vending machines openly displayed on streets and in public places, available at any time of the day or night.

In an interview with Dr. Malcom Tottie at Sweden's National Board of Health, I asked why there is an increase of venereal diseases in spite of the sex education and free and effective medical facilities.

Tottie said that the situation is puzzling and hard to explain. He offered these comments however:

> One answer is to be found in the changed social situation of Sweden. The trend of people moving from the country to the cities has been growing considerably these last years. In the cities the possibilities of unknown contacts are much more frequent and consequently more hazardous to the individual. The capacities of our health service has unfortunately diminished the dread of venereal disease, as the men of the medical profession, including myself, have informed the public about the efficient new methods of treatment now available.
>
> A psychological factor of importance is the fact that the publicity given to venereal disease is not necessarily followed by greater prudence by those concerned; people very often seem to go contrary to their own interests.

As shown in Table 17, the current wave of syphilis in Sweden is small compared with the rates before the early forties, when the effectiveness of penicillin was discovered.

Most persons contracting venereal disease in Sweden are young. Linner reports on a study of 135 gonorrhea patients for whom "the average age for the 80 women was 17.2, while that for the 55 men was 18.3. One-fourth of the total were children of divorced parents and more than 40 per cent had had previous contact with the child welfare board [an agency which treats cases of juvenile delinquents].[34]

Abortions

In 1965 there were 6,669 applications for legal abortions, of which 6,208 were granted.[35] In 1965, 54 illegal abortions were "known to the police."[36] There is no way of knowing how many illegal abortions occur. Linner states that yearly estimates range from 5,000 to 20,000.[37]

The present law on abortion went into effect in 1939, with modifications in 1946 and 1963. A woman can obtain a legal abortion under five different circumstances: if childbirth would endanger her life; if childbirth would seriously undermine her health; if she is pregnant because of rape or incest; if there is reason to believe either parent may transmit a form of insanity, serious disease, or serious handicap; if the fetus has been injured so that disease or deformity may be expected. Abortion is not available as a means of birth control, that is, it cannot be had simply because a woman does not want to have a child.

There is presently considerable controversy in Sweden about the possibility of making abortion available to any woman who wants it. Some women's groups see the right to abortion as a key issue in equal rights between the sexes. An editorial in *Dagens Nyheter* has spoken out against the double standard, saying that both the child and the mother will suffer if a woman is forced to bear and raise a child against her will.[38]

Until 1967 all fifty states of the United States declared abortion to be a crime except when necessary to save the mother's life and, in a few cases, when necessary to preserve her health. "In actual practice many doctors have been stretching, twisting, and torturing the law to fit what they regard as real medical needs. . . ."[39] Most of the extralegal abortions in hospitals are available only for well-to-do women, whereas women without means must search out the bleak and inferior facilities of quacks and amateur abortionists. It is variously estimated that 200,000 to 1.2 million illegal abortions occur in the United States each year.[40] Approximately 10,000 legal abortions occur each year.

In early 1967 the American Medical Association polled doctors on abortion. Of 40,089 who returned the questionnaire, 86.9 per cent favored liberalization of abortion laws.[41] Later in 1967 the A.M.A. loosened its 94-year-old policy, which limited abortion to cases where the mother's life was in danger. It stated a new policy favoring laws which sanction abortion "when pregnancy threatens the life or health of the mother, when the fetus is in grave danger of being deformed or mentally retarded, or in pregnancies resulting from legally established rape or incest."[42] This follows the Scandinavian pattern.

Before the A.M.A.'s action, three states—Colorado, California, and North Carolina—had reformed their abortion laws. Since that time the "model law" suggested by the A.M.A. has been debated in most of the state legislatures. In a number of states the model law has been defeated; in several states the issue is pending. New York State has passed a law leaving the decision on abortion to the doctor and the pregnant woman; depending on how the doctors respond, this law may be more liberal than the abortion law of Sweden.

MARRIAGE AND DIVORCE

Late marriages have been traditional in Sweden. Only in recent decades has there been a trend toward somewhat earlier marriages. In 1941-1945 the average age of men at first marriage was 28.7 and women 26.1. In 1967 the average age of first marriage of men was 25.9 and of women 23.3

The average of first marriage in the United States in 1967 was 23.1 for men and 20.6 for women. The age of first marriage in the United States has been going down since 1890, and the percentage of teenage marriages is higher than in other industrial countries.[43] The "romantic complex" has made marriage seem all-important in the United States.

When a premarital pregnancy occurs in the United States, there is pressure to hurry the marriage. Illegitimacy in the United States implies more disgrace than in Sweden. "It is perhaps typically Swedish," says Linner, "that many of those who become pregnant prior to marriage are not forced into an undesired marriage." Only about 40 per cent of parents of children born out of wedlock marry.

Divorce

The divorce rate in Sweden has been increasing in recent decades, as indicated in Table 19. The divorce-marriage ratio has been computed for each year by calculating the number of divorces which occurred for every 100 marriages in the same year. This index has many shortcomings, but it is the most meaningful index available. In the last ten years there has been approximately one divorce in the United States for every four marriages and approximately one divorce in Sweden for every six marriages. In the 1930's and early 1940's the United States rate was about

TABLE 19

No. of Divorces Per 100 Marriages, 1867-1967, Sweden and United States.

Year	Sweden	U.S.	Year	Sweden	U.S.	Year	Sweden	U.S.
1867	.6	2.8	1930	5.1	17.0	1949	13.8	25.1
1887	.9	5.5	1931	5.5	17.3	1950	14.8	23.1
1900	1.3	7.9	1932	5.9	16.3	1951	15.5	23.9
1910	1.9	8.8	1933	5.9	15.0	1952	15.4	25.5
1915	2.6	10.4	1934	5.6	15.7	1953	15.8	18.8
1916	2.7	10.6	1935	5.3	16.4	1954	16.2	25.4
1917	2.9	10.6	1936	5.3	17.2	1955	16.8	24.7
1918	2.8	11.6	1937	5.6	17.5	1956	16.6	24.2
1919	2.9	12.3	1938	5.9	18.5	1957	16.9	25.2
1920	3.0	13.4	1939	5.8	18.3	1958	17.0	25.7
1921	3.5	13.7	1940	5.9	16.9	1959	17.5	26.4
1922	4.0	13.1	1941	6.1	17.3	1960	17.7	25.8
1923	4.1	13.4	1942	6.6	18.1	1961	16.6	26.7
1924	4.5	14.4	1943	7.6	22.8	1962	16.4	26.2
1925	4.7	14.8	1944	8.4	27.5	1963	15.9	25.9
1926	4.9	15.0	1945	10.1	30.1	1964	15.7	26.1
1927	5.0	16.0	1946	11.0	26.6	1965	15.9	26.8
1928	5.1	16.6	1947	11.8	24.2	1966	16.8	20.0
1929	5.2	16.3	1948	11.7	22.3	1967	18.8	20.3

Sources for U.S.: 1867-1950 from W. F. Ogburn & M. F. Nimkoff, **Technology and the Changing Family** (New York: Houghton Mifflin, 1955); Ogburn and Nimkoff used a variety of census and vital statistics reports for computing these rates. 1951-67 computed from marriage and divorce totals in **Vital Statistics of the United States,** Vol. 3, Tables 1-1, 2-1.

Sources for Sweden: 1867-1934 computed from **Historical Abstracts of Sweden,** Part I: **Population,** Tables B2, B8. 1935-50 computed from marriage and divorce data, **Demographic Yearbook 1951** (New York: United Nations), Tables 24, 26. 1950-53 computed from **Demographic Yearbook 1954,** Table 34. 1954-62 computed from **Demographic Yearbook 1963,** Table 29. 1963-67 computed from **Statistical Abstract of Sweden 1968,** Tables 38, 40.

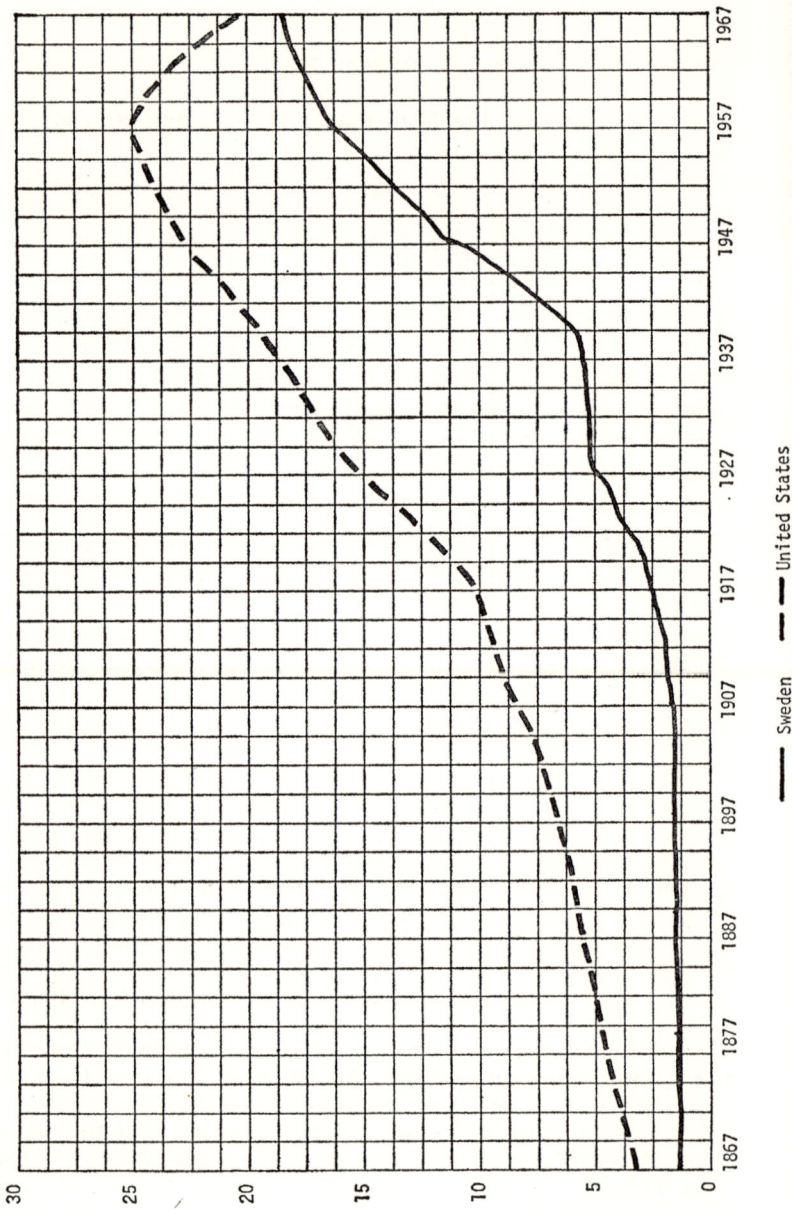

Figure 5: Sweden and United States Divorce rates compared. (Rates-Number of Divorces per 100 Marriages Occuring in Given Years.)

—— Sweden   – – United States

three times as high as that of Sweden. In the 1950's and the early 1960's the rate for the United States has been about 50 per cent higher than that of Sweden. In the last few years the rates have moved close together. Figure 5 compares the trends for Sweden and the United States.

Increased divorce in Sweden seems to relate to socio-economic changes similar to those of the United States: more urbanism and an increased number of industrial jobs as contrasted with the rural living and farming of an earlier day; an increased social and geographical mobility; more freedom for women.

Divorce rates by themselves do not tell us much about the relative amount of family stability which exists in a given society. They do not reveal how serious the social break in a marriage has to be before there is resort to divorce. They give no clue to the amount of desertion and other forms of family disruption. Nor do they reveal the problems in the aftermath of divorce.

At the present time, however, divorce rates are the only indices of family instability available for comparisons between the United States and Sweden.

Most societies permit more premarital than extramarital sex freedom. Premarital sex involves less deception and may even be considered a preparation for marriage. Extramarital freedom, however, generally does involve deception of a kind which makes a mockery of the marriage contract.

Sweden is no exception to this generalization. Ninety-three per cent of the married persons in the Zetterberg study said they disapproved of extramarital sex. Ninety-five per cent of them stated they had not had extramarital relations within a year. This does not mean that they have never had such relations. But Zetterberg thinks marital infidelity is very low and that it is not increasing.[44]

Davis has stated:

> . . . the fact that premarital intercourse on the part of girls is an accepted practice in Scandinavian countries does not mean that the family is "disappearing" or is "bankrupt" in those countries. On the contrary, one gets the impression that the Swedish or Norwegian family is somehow a more viable institution, certainly one more adapted to modern conditions, than the typical

Latin-American family, where the wives and daughters of the upper and middle classes are sedulously "protected" while the daughters of the lower class are used for concubines, prostitutes, and "servants."[45]

The relatively low rate of "forced marriages" in Sweden probably keeps the divorce rate lower than it would otherwise be. A similar effect stems from the fact that engagements are traditionally long in Sweden. Many individuals engage in a kind of "trial marriage" in which a couple live together for a time, intending perhaps to marry but breaking up before marriage takes place. Some persons have a number of such arrangements before marriage. When marriage does take place, one would suppose that the participants have more certainty about their marital choices than they might otherwise have had.

About 20 per cent of the population never marries. (In the U.S. the figure is 10 per cent.) It is not known whether the people who make up this 20 per cent would have been more divorce-prone had they married as compared with those who do not marry, but one may hypothesize that some of them stay out of marriage because they are not the kinds of persons who would adjust to married living. Some may not wish to give up the non-marital sexual freedom. When other conditions are similar, one may assume that divorce rates will generally be lower in societies where the number of persons who never marry is greatest.

Divorce in Sweden does not require some kind of "fault" in one of the marital partners. Swedish law does not require that one party be proved "guilty," as if the divorce proceedings

TABLE 20

Divorces in Sweden, 1957, 1962, 1967, Classified by Related Factors

Year	Divorce After 1-year Separation	Divorce After 3 Years of Separation Due to Dissension	Adultery	Condemnation in Criminal Trial	Drunkenness	Mental Disease	Other	Total Divorce
1957	7,091	441	1,097	30	89	71	37	8,856
1962	7,056	426	1,186	27	105	31	16	8,847
1967	8,656	431	1,483	24	82	25	21	10,722

Source: Adapted from **Statistical Abstract of Sweden, 1968,** Table 40.

constituted a kind of criminal trial where all the accusations and evidence are displayed in public. It is enough for the couple simply to be agreed that they want a divorce.

Except in a few states "mutual consent" is not a legal basis for divorce in the United States, where one party must be accused and in effect judged guilty if divorce is to be justified.

Attempts are made in Sweden to save a marriage wherever possible. But there is no supposition that all marriages can be saved; there are couples who are quite irreconcilable, and immediate termination of the marriage is recognized as the only solution. However, the majority of couples applying for divorce are forced to consider it for a while in a kind of test divorce—a legal separation. This arrangement is comparatively easy to make. The couple need only hand the court a joint application stating they are unable to live together on grounds of "long and unreconcilable incompatibility." They are not required to prove their incompatibility in court. The couple meet with a mediator appointed by the court, and the court makes the decree of separation.

If, during the test divorce, the couple realize they acted hastily, they can revalidate their marriage simply by living together again. If after a year of separation they still want a divorce, as they usually do, they can file a new petition for divorce. Often all matters, such as custody of the children, alimony, and property arrangements, are agreed on before they get into the court, and the court only confirms the agreements.

In 1967, 12,201 legal separations and 10,722 divorces were granted. Of the divorces, 8,656 were granted to couples who had been separated for a year and 431 to couples who had been separated for three years.[46]

CONTROVERSY

A Swedish housewife who had spent several years in the United States as a student said, "In the United States people are furtive about their sex life. In Sweden we are more open about it and we are not plagued with a sense of guilt. We debate sex issues without embarrassment."

The ongoing controversy reveals the presence of trends and

countertrends in sex behavior; it reveals, to varying degrees, that not all sex behavior presently found in Sweden is approved by all groups in the population.

There is opposition from the conservative elements within the Lutheran state church, to which more than 90 per cent of the people belong. In 1951 the thirteen bishops of Sweden formulated a conservative statement on sex and marriage. They pronounced all sex before or outside of marriage to be a sin against God. Except under limited circumstances in marriage, they rejected the notion of contraceptives and birth control. The bishops' position has been heavily criticized, but it has not been modified.

The bishops' position has produced an angry dispute within the church. Carl Gustaf Boethius, editor of the church's magazine, *Our Church*, declared the bishops were wrong when they insisted that sex belongs only within marriage. He explained that ". . . in reality, there are many young couples not yet married who are living together and are not acting immorally." Seven hundred forty-four pastors wrote to the church's Central Board demanding that Boethius be dismissed. The Board refused, saying that free discussion should prevail.[47]

The conservative view of many pastors is expressed by Rev. Claes Robach of a large parish in Stockholm. He believes that sex relations outside marriage are always wrong:

> If people are stealing, the government wouldn't say stealing is right. We should have a good sexual education which gives the facts needed about reproduction and pregnancy. But it should be done in the framework that monogamous marriage is the only normal situation for sex relations. And it should say abstinence is healthy and the only sure prevention from fertilization. [Pastor Robach fears sex education in the schools may become a way in which teachers shape the minds and morals of children.] The strong stress on sex education just now is because there are some forces that want to leave Christian morality. They want to say you should not be prevented by any commandments from God or man from having sexual experience.

Most ministers are not this traditional. Rev. Ingmar Strom, director of the Lutheran Church's Central Board, thinks the church should not be dogmatic in condemning premarital sex relations. He thinks there are good reasons for abstinence, "but they are not as strong as they used to be." He thinks that in some situations sex relations for young unmarried couples should be approved "because it is worse if they have to wait years until they can have a home of their own and marriage."[49]

It should be added that the opposition of the church authorities to sex outside marriage carries little weight with most Swedish people. Swedes, particularly the young, frequently say that the attitude of the church is irrelevant and passé because the church has not related itself to modern society. Although over 90 per cent of the people belong to the state Lutheran Church, it is generally estimated that on any given Sunday only 2 to 4 per cent of them attend church. For the most part the churches are empty.

Nearly all adolescents do go through training for confirmation. A medical doctor told me, "No, we do not attend church; but this does not mean the church has no influence over us; we never forget our confirmation."

In 1964 a group of 140 doctors signed a petition to the government warning of the spread of promiscuity and urging the schools to teach "firmer sex norms." They condemned premarital sex as being a "danger to the nation." Most of the nation's doctors, however, did not agree.[50]

What is the attitude of the educational authorities concerning sexual freedom for youth?

"The university exercises no moral control over the student," said Teddy Brunius, a faculty member at the university in Uppsala. "There is nothing that distinguishes a student from an ordinary wage earner. He takes his meals where he likes. He is at liberty to drink alcoholic liquors and have sexual relations, if he does so within the law. In short, the student is independent."[51]

A graduate coed stated that she has lived in student housing for several years.

> The formal rules of the university housing authorities [she said] are against unmarried students living together. However, they say nothing when it is done and there are couples doing

this all the time. Visiting between men and women in the privacy of their rooms is also a common practice. Visiting is not always for the purpose of sex relations. Student visiting serves a social function and sometimes it means studying together when they are enrolled in the same courses. Men and women students frequently live in the same dormitories although generally on separate floors or wings.

Connery quotes a Swedish educator as saying, "Is it fair for society to insist that young people spend more and more years at their studies, often into their middle twenties, and to remain 'pure' at the very time of their greatest sexual drive?"[52]

A Reuters news story from the sessions of the World Council of Churches at Uppsala in July, 1968, tells about a news conference on sex presented at the request of visiting Americans. "A pretty 22-year-old brunette, Aarin Rhonde, was astonished by an American newsman's question about the attitude of Swedish university authorities regarding unmarried student couples living together.

" 'What has it to do with them, what students do in their private lives?' Miss Rhonde asked."

She explained that student living quarters are managed by the student union. If a couple do live together, they have to sign a contract agreeing to give up the larger quarters if they split up.

Sweden has required sex education in all nine grades of the public schools since 1957. Instruction in the biological and social significance of sex start in the earliest grades, and educational authorities think it should start in the home before that.

An official *Handbook on Sex Instruction in Swedish Schools* was published by the Swedish Board of Education in 1957. This lays down some general guidelines for teachers of sex education.

The Handbook takes a conservative approach on premarital sex relations. Thus in a sample lesson for students 14 to 16 years old, the Handbook advises the teacher to tell her pupils, "At your age, and in general while you are still growing up, you should not engage in sexual relations. You ought to live a life of continence during the years while you are growing up." A moral tone of this kind runs throughout the book. Some biology texts used in sex education reflect a similar view. One 9th-grade biology text, for example, states, "Since young boys and girls should not have sexual relations, they should not use contraceptives either."

The moralistic approach to sex education has its outspoken critics. Birgitta Linner, Stockholm marriage counselor and author of *Sex and Society in Sweden,* for example, says it must be accepted that sex relations prevail among the young and that moralizing will not abolish such relations. She believes the purpose of sex education is, of course, not that of stimulating sex relations for the young. However, the reality of sex activities among the young must be recognized. Linner thinks that the best hope is to help youth, through education, to develop a sense of responsibility concerning how, with whom, and under what circumstances sex relations may ethically take place.

Other critics of the sex-education program maintain that many teachers are inadequately trained for their roles. Some think that teaching the use of contraceptives and making them freely available will only increase the amount of casual sex relations. There are some parents who believe that all sex education for their children should take place in the home.

Zetterberg found that only 9 per cent of his sample opposed sex education in the schools and that 5 per cent were uncertain about it. The great majority favored it. His study also revealed that about a third of the schoolchildren did not receive sex instruction in schools where teachers and schools still avoided it.[53]

It is sometimes said that the sex behavior of Swedish youth is really no different from that of American youth except that what many Swedes do openly and without guilt the Americans do secretly and with guilt. Such a statement has a certain amount of truth in it, but it does not cover all the dimensions of the question. Because of the differences in historical backgrounds and because puritanical ideas stemming from the Calvinistic ethic never achieved as powerful a grip on Sweden as they did on the United States, as well as a complex variety of the other chance factors, the Swedes do not equate morality and certain forms of sex behavior to the same degree as do Americans. This difference was pointed up by a Swedish coed who said she could not see what sex has to do with morals.

When a prominent American clergyman visited Sweden in 1955, he stated that "morals in Scandinavia are very low. I wouldn't say they are alarmingly low—but they are low—particularly sexual morality."[54] When this statement was made, there was no acknowledgement of the high standards of honesty in business and in government, nor of the low rates of violence and theft in Sweden. The clergyman did not even recognize that a considerable amount of premarital sex is responsible behavior. He only learned that premarital sex is extensive in Sweden, and since he believed such behavior is sinful, he pronounced Swedish morals to be low. It seems peculiarly American that the chief connotations of the word "morals" are sexual.

All societies have mores about sex relations because of the necessity of seeing that children born of such relations are cared for. In all societies there is a certain amount of concern for the stability of the family, since the family is the chief agency of child care and training.

However, there are no mores which are absolute to all cultures, and this is evident when one compares Sweden and the United States. Although there are similarities in sex behavior and norms between the two countries, there are also considerable differences. The urban-industrial environment is similar in the two countries, but the historical backgrounds are very different. Certain kinds of premarital sex have long been taken for granted in Sweden with little or no evidence of guilt. Controversy prevails in Sweden, but the forces condemning the freedom of sex are relatively ineffectual.

NOTES

1. David Jenkins, *Sweden and the Price of Progress* (New York: Coward, McCann, 1968), p. 202.

2. For an account of peasant courting and sex customs before modern times see Alva Myrdal, *Nation and Family* (New York: Harper, 1941); new M.I.T. paperback edition, 1968, pp. 42-47.

3. Reuters news release as written by Stephen Croll, July 17, 1968.

4. Fredric Fleisher, *The New Sweden* (New York: McKay, 1967), p. 259.

5. Anna-Lisa Kälvesten, *The Social Structure of Sweden* (Stockholm: Swedish Institute, 1966).

6. *Ibid.*, p. 32.

7. Reported by Birgitta Linner, *Sex and Society in Sweden* (New York: Random House, 1967), p. 18.

8. *Ibid.*, p. 19. Used by permission.

9. *On Sexual Life in Sweden,* to be published by Bedford Press; the present quotations are based on a summary by J. Robert Moskin, *Look,* "The New Contraceptive Society," Feb. 4, 1969, pp. 50, 53.

10. *Ibid.*, p. 50.

11. *Ibid.*, p. 50.

12. *Linner*, p. 26.

13. Connery, *The Scandinavians* (New York: Simon & Schuster, 1966), pp. 45, 314 f. Used by permission.

14. Alfred C. Kinsey & others, *Sexual Behavior in the Human Female* (Phila.: Saunders), p. 291.

15. Robert R. Bell, *Premarital Sex in a Changing Society* (Englewood Cliffs, N.J.: Prentice-Hall, 1966), p. 58.

16. Kinsey, p. 291.

17. Bell, p. 57.

18. Kinsey, p. 316.

19. Bell, p. 101.

20. Ira L. Reiss, *Social Context of Premarital Sexual Permissiveness* (New York: Holt, Rinehart & Winston, 1967), p. 116.

21. *Ibid.*, p. 113.

22. *Ibid.*, pp. 124 f.

23. Harold T. Christensen & George R. Carpenter, "Value-Behavior Discrepancies Regarding Premarital Coitus in Three Western Cultures," *American Sociological Review,* Vol. 27 (Feb., 1962), pp. 66-74.

24. *International Journal of Comparative Sociology,* Vol. 3 (1962), pp. 124-37.

25. The *Penal Code* of Sweden, Chap. 6, Sec. 8.

26. Frank Murray in an Associated Press story, Des Moines *Register,* June 29, 1969.

27. *Statistical Abstract of Sweden, 1968,* Table 42.

28. Zetterberg, p. 50.

29. *Trends in Illegitimacy, United States, 1940-1965,* U.S. Dept. of Health, Education, and Welfare, Series 21, No. 5, p. 2.

30. *Ibid.*

31. Linner, p. 86.

32. *Statistical Abstract of Sweden, 1968,* Table 304.

33. *Venereal Disease Fact Sheet, 1967,* U.S. Dept. of Health, Education, and Welfare, p. 2.

34. Linner, pp. 89 f.

35. *Statistical Abstract of Sweden, 1967,* Table 294.

36. *Ibid.,* Table 295.

37. Linner, p. 75.

38. David Sternberg, "Sweden Debates Sex Morality," *American Scandinavian Review,* Vol. LIV, No. 1 (Mar., 1966), pp. 37-43.

39. New York *Times,* Jan. 8, 1968.

40. *Medical World News,* Sept. 29, 1967, p. 49.

41. New York *Times,* Jan. 8, 1968.

42. "Rewriting the Law on Abortion," *Medical World News,* Sept. 29, 1967, p. 46.

43. W. F. Ogburn & M. F. Nimkoff, *Technology and the Changing Family* (Boston: Houghton Mifflin), pp. 58-70.

44. Moskin, *Look,* Feb. 4, 1969, p. 53.

45. Kingsley Davis, "Sexual Behavior," *Contemporary Social Problems,* ed. Robert K. Merton & Robert A. Nisbet (New York: Harcourt, Brace & World, 1966), p. 369.

46. *Statistical Abstract of Sweden, 1968,* Table 38.

47. "Sweden's New Battle Over Sex," *Look,* Nov. 15, 1966, pp. 36-42.

48. *Ibid.,* pp. 41 f.

49. *Ibid.,* p. 42.

50. Fleisher, pp. 259 f.

51. Donald Connery, "Scandinavian Youth," *Holiday,* Nov., 1966, pp. 115, 124.

52. Connery, *Scandinavians,* p. 40.

53. Moskin, *Look,* Feb. 4, 1969, p. 53.

54. Lester Davis, "The Controversy Over Swedish Morals," *Coronet,* Dec., 1956, p. 127.

VIII

Conclusions

We come back to the questions with which we started. Is deviant behavior rampant in Sweden? If so, is there a causal linkage between deviant behavior and the welfare system?

There is deviant behavior in Sweden, but its dimensions are within bounds; it is not threatening a dissolution or disorganization of Swedish society. There is no evidence that any of the several varieties of deviant behavior is a result of the social welfare program. If anything, welfarism diminishes, controls or prevents deviant behavior.

Critics who see a causal relationship between state welfarism and deviant behavior should be aware that there are many socioeconomic factors in modern societies which may relate causally to increased deviant behavior when it occurs.

MODERN SOCIETY AND DEVIANCE

Individuals in modern society frequently are members of many groups whose norms vary and sometimes are in direct conflict with one another. One may, for example, be a member of the military and also of some religious group which has strong strains of pacifism. Moreover, individuals are members not only of small locality and kinship groups but also of vast associations linked with interests of business or work. In addition, individuals are members of the vast complex collectivity called the state or nation.

No one has ever found a small non-industrial and non-urban society where harmony pervades all human relations and discord and deviance do not exist. One would suppose, however, that social control in small, relatively static, and more or less self-contained societies would be more effective, and deviant behavior less prevalent, than in complex modern societies. In traditional societies individuals are socialized more easily, with habits and values which are in line with social customs. Conformity to existing customs and social values is more readily built into personalities from the earliest years as contrasted with a modern complex society. When there is little social change, the child can see the nature of his future life in the life of his parents—the boy in that of his father, the girl in that of her mother. The boy grows gradually into the father's roles in work, in family, and in community life; very early he begins to assist his father, or in some cases the oldest male relative on his mother's side. He grows into his adult roles with a minimum of discontinuity. The same principle holds for the girl and the acquisition of her adult roles. One would expect that in such a society proper ways of behaving seem more or less natural and spontaneous and do not have to be coerced.

We expect social control in the small traditional society to be mostly of a personal kind. Impersonal coercion and violent techniques, with the use of police and jails, are at a minimum. Personal pressures by neighbors and relatives, gossip, ridicule, and praise probably suffice in most instances to prevent excessive deviant behavior and to produce the desired conduct. The individual member's desire for status and reputation, and the lack of subcultures in which deviant behavior can find approval, help maintain the social order. In such societies kinship is heavily emphasized and there is a strong attachment to the land, so that the kinship-locality group is almost the all-inclusive group in which personality develops and finds expression.

Although primitive cities appeared as early as five thousand years ago in Mesopotamia and Egypt, urbanism did not become a significant social force until recent times. In 1800 less than 10 per cent of the population of England and Wales lived in cities of 100,000 or more, while in 1951, 38.4 per cent lived in such cities. In 1900, 35 per cent lived in cities of 20,000 or more; by 1951, 69.3 per cent lived in cities of this size and 80.7 per cent lived in urban areas.

Only 5.1 per cent of the population of the United States lived in urban places in 1790. By 1850 the urban population was still only 13.5 per cent of the total population. However, in 1900 it was 39 per cent, and in 1920 the urban population outnumbered the rural population with 51.2 per cent of the total. In 1960 the United States census classified 69.9 per cent of the population as urban.[1]

Urbanization in Sweden is more recent, but its rate of growth has been much more rapid. In 1900, 22 per cent of the population lived in cities. In 1950 the corresponding figure was 46 per cent and in 1965, 77 per cent.[2]

Industrialization has had the same explosive growth as urbanism and has been closely allied with it. We have previously noted that industrialism came to Sweden relatively late. However, when it came it expanded rapidly.

An overview of the social effect of industrialization relevant to deviant behavior should include the following:

1. Large numbers of people have migrated out of rural areas to cities, where, in advanced industrial countries, they outnumber the farm population.

2. A high degree of work specialization made possible by a "wide market" has wiped out self-sufficient parochial economies. Specialization by workers and industries increases the area of interdependence, making for large complex societies in which the norms of business and government play a larger role than ever before.

3. Industrial societies are dynamic. A stable or relatively static equilibrium cannot endure for long. Socio-economic changes become continuous when a huge complex of industrial culture exists, and these changes tend to carry over into other aspects of society.

4. The Industrial Revolution has witnessed a steady growth in the size of factories and industrial concerns. Such growth has been facilitated by more complex machines and by diversified and mobile sources of mechanical power, as well as by new organizational and engineering techniques. Modern society has become "organizational" society. It has vast networks of impersonal bureaucracies, not only in the economy and in government but

also in the large voluntary organizations which serve religious, educational and other social and "cultural" functions.

All of this is not to suggest that there is a rigid economic determinism which directly produces more deviant behavior. Even the simplest societies are characterized by a variety of deviant behavior; alcoholism, for example, seems to be characteristic of nearly all societies. It is to say, however, that the industrial-urban complex has added some highly significant new dimensions to the problems of deviant behavior. These changes in social life are considerably more relevant to the increase of deviant behavior than is state welfarism. In fact, welfare measures can generally be seen as efforts to protect some of the less fortunate individuals and families from some of the ravages and insecurities of the new ways of life.

5. Modern complex societies, with their vast areas pervaded by anonymous relations, make detection and reporting of certain offenses more difficult. Geographical and social mobility takes many individuals out of one social context and places them in others where social norms for behavior differ and where social control is made more difficult. Moreover, large urban areas have made possible permanent subcultures of delinquency, theft, and rackets.

Very few people, if any, in the large modern society find it possible to live out their entire lives in one all-inclusive locality-kinship group. Most people find themselves in a number of groups, a condition which can be personally enriching but which may also mean that life is more likely to be segmented. Some special problems are created if the groups have diverse norms so that one cannot be loyal to one group without being disloyal to others.

6. Finally, nearly all the deviant behavior which sociologists analyze—alcoholism, use of narcotic drugs, delinquency, suicide, functional mental disorders, sex offenses, prejudice, discrimination, crime—is no longer a concern of local groups only; such behavior involves the large collectives of cities, states, and nations. There is relatively less effectiveness of such personal controls as praise for approved behavior and scorn and mockery for disapproved behavior. Although we know that intimate associations do exist in

urban areas, city life often does make it difficult for individuals to become psychologically close. Kinship ties may be attenuated and next-door neighbors often scarcely know each other. With less possibility of personal types of social control, police, fines, jails, and prisons more or less take their place, though generally with only limited effectiveness.

DEVIANT BEHAVIOR IN SWEDEN IN PERSPECTIVE

Crime

Crime rates have been increasing in Sweden as they have in other Western countries. With the rapid growth of industrialism there have come more social complexities which require more laws and more types of social control. More automobiles on highways, for example, require an increasing number of regulations, some of which will be broken. Automobiles also are fairly easily stolen.

Industrialism has brought higher standards of living. With widespread affluence as never before, one would suppose there would be less need and less pressure to steal. However, stealing is seldom a simple matter of desire for the necessities of life. Many peasants in traditional societies seem relatively honest in spite of their poverty. Affluence, however, displays a wide variety of goods before people who may feel increasingly severe pressures to attain higher standards of living.

The crime problem in Sweden obviously does not have the dimensions of the crime problem in the United States. Sweden has almost no violence. It has several important advantages in crime control. It has a relatively homogeneous population, a nationwide integrated police force, no city ghettos, and a welfare-oriented correctional system. It has no crime syndicates which buy off local police and government officials and which operate massive rackets as in the United States.

Alcoholism

Sweden has a problem with alcohol, and the Swedes are acutely aware of it. There has been a long history of abusive drinking and a wet-dry political struggle similar to that in the United States. However, the drinking problem antedated the welfare state by many years. The present educational program regarding the problems of alcohol use is largely the endeavor of the welfare state. This is also true of the various public institutions for alcoholics and the community Temperance Boards.

The pattern of drinking in Sweden is changing even as in the United States. Less alcohol per capita is being consumed than in earlier times even though a larger portion of the population is drinking than in earlier times. In 1968 the amount of pure alcohol consumed, from all sources, per inhabitant 15 years and over, was 1.7 gallons compared with 2.1 gallons in 1861. The per capita consumption is considerably less than in a number of other European countries.

The style of drinking is changing from "all-out Nordic binges" to one that involves more spacing of drinks and more drinking with eating. An increasing use of wine and beer, and less spirits, is also facilitating more temperance. The welfare state through its control of the traffic in alcoholic beverages is fostering a change in the drinking patterns to make them more suitable to the technological and organizational requirements of the urban-industrial age. More wine and beer and less distilled beverages is also facilitating a more temperate approach to alcohol use.

Drugs

In recent years a rash of drug abuse has appeared in Sweden, especially among children and young people. There is no meaningful way by which this can be attributed to the welfare state, which was well developed before drug abuse became a problem. Moreover, similar patterns of drug abuse have appeared in other countries, such as Italy and Spain, which place little emphasis on welfarism. Drug abuse, particularly addiction to opium and its extracts and preparations, such as morphine and heroin, had become a serious problem in the United States in the 19th century. The abuse of heroin continues to be a serious problem in the United States, particularly in the big-city ghettos. There is almost no problem at all in Sweden with heroin, and there is no Mafia-like organization involved in international traffic in hard drugs.

The urban-industrial age emphasizes the use of new products and new ways of doing things. Drug abuse may be one of the many possible fads which some youth feel they must give a try. Moreover, developments in chemistry have made certain stimulant and narcotic drugs available for the first time—which in itself is not a cause for their use but is a necessary condition.

Suicide

The notion that the paternalism of the welfare state causes higher suicide rates cannot be supported either by evidence or by any logical argument. Both Sweden and Norway have extensive welfare measures, but Norway has a low suicide rate, about half that of Sweden. Norway is still largely a country of fishing and agricultural villages and scattered homesteads, while Sweden is heavily industrialized and urbanized with greater possibilities that individuals will become socially isolated.

Some critics allege that boredom and laziness cause suicide. But ennui and lack of incentive are not general conditions in Sweden. Work addiction and anxiety to get ahead is far more evident than indolence and lack of initiative. This is particularly true among middle and upper classes, where suicide rates are highest.

Dr. M. L. Farber, who has spent time in Denmark and Norway in a study of suicide, has cited "two theoretical principles to support the idea that the welfare state has at least a mildly ameliorative effect on suicide. First, suicide is a 'consequence of experienced deprivation' not blamable on a type of government that supplies the opposite of deprivation; and second, the welfare state provides a hopeful future outlook in which economic anxieties are reduced."[3]

"I have never encountered a man who attempted suicide because he had just received a social security check," Farber states.

Farber warns against the "fallacy of assuming a causal linkage" when one finds a high suicide rate in a welfare state: "In these states, as in non-welfare states, there are many other factors such as increased urbanization, technological change, industrialization and changes in work activities that may well influence people with damaged personalities to do away with themselves."

Farber asserts that with the social legislation of the New Deal the suicide rate in the United States dropped from the relatively high rates of the 1920's and early 1930's. He also notes that the rate in the Canadian province of Saskatchewan, which has many welfare provisions, is "slightly lower than that of its neighboring Provinces. . . ."

Sex and Marriage

Much of what Americans think of as deviant sexual behavior is not so defined in Sweden. Premarital sex relations, especially when tied to courting and engagement situations, were generally approved in peasant society in pre-modern Sweden and are still considered acceptable.

In recent decades casual and promiscuous sex relations have had an increase due, among other things, to far more contacts between the sexes in the urban setting and to readily available means of birth control. The large middle classes, however, prefer steady relations between the sexes, relations which involve mutuality and responsibility.

High illegitimacy rates in Sweden are not new, as if brought on by welfare measures. Thus the rates were somewhat higher in the late 1920's, when welfare services were very limited, than in the late 1960's, when welfare services were elaborate and complete. Jenkins asserts that a hundred years ago, when there were no state welfare measures at all, "more than 40 per cent of all children born in Stockholm were borne by unwed mothers."[4] In 1860 the average annual urban rate of illegitimacy in Sweden was 25 per cent of all children born, as compared with the present rate of about 15 per cent.

Divorce rates in Sweden have been considerably lower than those in the United States. Only in the past few years has the rate in Sweden approached that of the United States. Rural and urban differences in divorce rates in Sweden have been considerable. The urban divorce rates per 100,000 population in the 1920's and 1930's, for example, were approximately four times the rates in rural areas.[5] Since welfarism is to be found in both country and city, it is evident that urban living, not welfarism, has been the important factor making for higher divorce rates.

* * *

The critics of Sweden have made many easy and superficial generalizations, usually with little or no evidence to back their statements. When they do cite evidence, it is generally irrelevant to the problem or is stacked to lead to unwarranted conclusions. For example, it can truthfully be said that the syphilis rate in Sweden in 1966 was almost five times as high as in 1960. But the rate in 1960 was very low (1.2 cases per 100,000 population), so that the rate in 1966, though higher than it should be, was only 5.5 cases per 100,000 population, a rate which is only one-fourth the rate which prevailed in the middle forties. Often critics seem to lack an understanding of the deviance rates in other countries, including their own. In 1966 the rate of syphilis in the United States was nearly double the rate which prevailed in Sweden in the same year.

Similarly, it can truthfully be said that the amount of robbery in Sweden "known to the police" increased 109 per cent between 1961 and 1967. Even so, the rate in 1967 was only 13.1 per 100,000 population, while the United States rate reported by the FBI was ten times as high.

Often the critics take data out of its social and historical context, giving misleading and alarming impressions. They generally fail to inform us where and how they obtain the evidence for what they assert. They make statements such as, "The police say that delinquency is getting out of hand," without telling us which police and how many police say this and how their opinions were discovered. Some critics quote "a leading psychiatrist" who blames suicide on welfarism without identifying the psychiatrist or indicating why he thinks this is so.

Of course, there is deviant behavior in Sweden. But it is not rampant. It is not so pervasive and serious that it threatens the breakdown of society or the disintegration of personality. When one lives in Sweden for a time, it becomes a mystery how and why the critics have built the stereotype of a society in great disrepair and near collapse, where individuals supposedly suffer a loss of nerve and lack of purpose. Swedish society is thoroughly organized with a thriving grass-roots democracy and widespread participation by people at all levels in both economic and political affairs.

Neither collectively nor on the individual level does Sweden suffer from a lack of objectives or present the appearance of breakdown.

NOTES

1. Urban population data from Kingsley, "The Origin and Growth of Urbanism in the World," *American Journal of Sociology,* Vol. LX, No. 5 (Mar., 1955), pp. 433 f.

2. Statistical Abstract of Sweden, 1967, Table 9.

3. Maurice L. Farber, "Welfare, Suicide Linked?" *Science News Letter,* Vol. 88, No. 7 (Aug. 14, 1965), p. 111.

4. David Jenkins, *Sweden and the Price of Progress* (New York: Coward-McCann, 1968), p. 17.

5. *Historical Statistics of Sweden,* Part I, Table B8.